When Professional Women Retire . . .

Food for Thought and Palate

To: Betsy

**Inga Wiehl and
Ellie Heffernan**

*The Good Life is
within you —

& Ellie

Wonderful friend
and hiking pal —

Love, Inga*

Hamilton Books
A member of
The Rowman & Littlefield Publishing Group, Inc.
Lanham · Boulder · New York · Toronto · Oxford

Copyright © 2005 by
Hamilton Books
4501 Forbes Boulevard
Suite 200
Lanham, Maryland 20706
UPA Acquisitions Department (301) 459-3366

PO Box 317
Oxford
OX2 9RU, UK

Library of Congress Control Number: 2004117054
ISBN 0-7618-3111-8 (paperback : alk. ppr.)

For our husbands and children,
who have shaped our lives,
as we have shaped theirs.

ഇൻ

CONTENTS

PREFACE

W hen *Professional Women Retire ... Food for Thought and Palate* focuses on the loss of professional identity with retirement and shows ways of transforming that outward loss to inward gain, a process resulting in the good life as we perceive it.

Our approach to the suggested transformation is philosophical, rather than prescriptive. We believe that by facing emotional and intellectual issues, we can work through them and arrive at a definition of "the good life" in the Third Stage, following those of childhood and employment years. Urging a thoughtful assessment of ourselves as retired professional women, we advocate finding a passion leading to tasks that will engage our attention and demand our commitment. To that end, we define and discuss five realms of endeavors in which such tasks may be carried out, evidenced by our own experience, stories told by women across the land, and numerous literary examples.

Predicating our definition of "the good life" on insights offered by an *examined* life, we discuss ways of engaging our minds via a variety of projects and endeavors. Because we know that good health is vital to a good life, we furthermore accord our stomachs some time and attention with favorite recipes in every chapter.

The *Tool Book* features not only a list of text references and recommended readings; it also offers a directory of agencies considered particularly helpful in posing, answering, or directing inquiries into part-time jobs, volunteer opportunities, continuing education, exercise options, or travel destinations and purposes. Finally, it provides a guide for use of the primary text in chautauquas, seminars, workshops, and focus groups.

In sum, this text is a celebration of women's ways of knowing how to retire into "the good life."

Inga Wiehl
Ellie Heffernan

1

FROM EMPLOYMENT TO RETIREMENT

We know no rule of procedure, we are voyagers,
discoverers of the not-known, the unrecorded; we have
no map; possibly we will reach haven, heaven.

— H.D. (Hilda Doolittle)
From "The Walls Do Not Fall."

All professional women will eventually retire, but each for her own reasons, in her own way, at her own time, and with her own concerns.

Some of us may feel "forced" to retire, pressured by expectations in our working fields, by our mates' desire for company as they enter the potentially most challenging phase of their lives, or by family needs or health issues demanding more time than our career lives will grant. Others may experience no pressures to retire but choose to do so because the time has come to explore other fields of work and engagement. The latter are the luckier ones: they are likely to have imagined what life could be in retirement and are eager to fashion and experience its options. Whether or not such imagined existences turn out as expected is at the time of retirement inconsequential because only the living out of this new phase can show its values and pitfalls, no matter how well imagined they may be. In fact, studies have shown that women's expectations of retirement often differ significantly from its reality and their lives in it.

Those of us who have not imagined or visualized a future in our Third Stage—following childhood and career life—may share Isak Dinesen's sentiment on her return to Denmark from Africa after the bankruptcy of marriage and coffee plantation. Those losses, she wrote, had sent her on a passage "outside the range of imagination but within the range of experience." Nor is our sense of loss unlike that of mothers who feel bereft of identity as the last child leaves home.

We suffer a sense of loss at giving up our careers because we have been heavily invested in our work and may realize that on retirement we have cancelled our membership in the market place yet retained our desire for the rewards such membership accrued. Like Shakespeare's King Lear, we have laid down the responsibilities of "professionalship" but lack the "readiness" to renounce the satisfactions professional employment confers. "I felt like being on a mountaintop and falling off," commented Anna Nassif, a retired professor of dance at the University of Wisconsin. "It needn't be like that, but that is the first realization that a very important part of your life is coming to a close."

A retiring physician felt the transition from employment to retirement "challenging" because of the personal investment she had made in her training and practice. "I'm going to turn my back on everything that I've learned," she wrote, "all the experience I've accumulated ... you really do close the door on your life." Yet another, a former university administrator, described the experience as "a defining moment," and a former associate dean felt retirement like "the rug is kind of feeling pulled out from under." For them, as for the rest of us, the question then arises of how, by what process, we may acquire readiness to renounce the satisfactions we know and build a life of potentially greater rewards in full accordance with our total identity, which is more encompassing than merely professional roles and the status they accord.

The experience of retiring is gradual and open ended. No ritual or meaningful ceremony—such as christenings, confirmations, weddings or school graduations—marks this critical transition in the life of an individual or hallows the date of severance from work and careers. Unlike those rituals, which are mostly planned and performed by elders guiding the celebrants, a retirement party is generally organized by colleagues who have not yet retired. They hold no road map to retirement land and cannot, therefore, be leaders into this new stage of life devoid of prescribed or socially generated roles. As Margaret Urban points out in *Mother Time*, "'Retirement,' unlike school and workplace, is not a place. It is not an activity, like education and work, nor a role defined by the development of skills or exercise of competence, like that of student or worker. Retirement is defined instead as the cessation of the adult role of worker."

Nor can former colleagues, however well intended, be expected to understand the needs of retirees or care deeply about the questions confronting us as we enter their ranks. Our own interest in those questions became acute only as we ourselves had to invent and frame the answers. "Old age is not interesting until one gets there," comments May Sarton's heroine Caro in *As We Are Now*. It is "a foreign country with an unknown language to the young, and even to the middle aged." Retirement parties, therefore, tend to focus on separation from past activities with little or no emphasis on moves into future engagements. Again, this is understandable in a milieu where neither the celebrant nor the celebrators have much of an idea—if any—what physical and mental adventure the future may hold.

A well-meant send-off, then, with nonetheless potentially negative overtones, may not fuel the energy it takes to sort out retirement issues and responsibilities, among them financial arrangements and health insurance needs. Those are practical matters craving attention and time, and for some, they remain primary concerns throughout their retirement years. Many professional women, however, are fortunate enough to have found resolutions for those issues via investments, pensions, and health care programs either self initiated or appended their careers. These women may therefore focus on generating an intellectual and emotional purpose for their lives, a supposition supported by a study conducted in 1991 by C. Ray Wingrove and Kathleen F.

Slevin. They researched the employment history of a group of professional women who had entered the world of work in the 1920's and 30's and thus pioneered the trend that did not fully emerge until the 1960's when women initiated careers after completing their college educations. We are fully aware, they wrote, that "our women are not typical of most female retirees either now or in the future. However, their lives do suggest what a *growing* minority of female retirees might be like in the next century, those who are educated, who have experienced uninterrupted careers in the labor force, who have enjoyed success in traditionally male professional and managerial positions and who retire with greater financial security and lives rich in friendships, activity and involvement." (Emphasis added)

"Friendships, activity and involvement" in this context are outcomes of generative thinking and feeling. What we are about to learn is that they demand a considered letting go of the past to invest in the future. That does not mean devaluing professional expertise, forgetting acquired lessons for living or ignoring the losses we incur as we let go of a hard forged and cherished professional identity. It does, however, pose a necessity for acknowledging the components of those losses as well as committing to their transformation. Our thinking at this time has made us conclude that professional identity was shaped, in individually varying degrees, by *the income we earned, the social status and contacts we generated*, and *the intellectual challenges we sought and met*.

On retirement, we must face and feel the loss of those in order that we may effect their transformation into gains for the phase of our lives we are about to begin. That phase, the Third Stage, has, as far as professional women are concerned, remained largely unresearched. We therefore enter that realm as into an unknown land partly because we have not read about it.

In contrast, the loss of identity experienced by many men as they retire has been well documented. Research has shown that men's identity is to a great extent fixed by the careers they pursue. Their intensity in that pursuit—equated with drive, seriousness and success—makes "cutting back" or "slowing down" difficult to accept. Those findings hold no surprise because, whether or not we are aware of it, custom and classical literature have acculturated us to accept them. Through our reading of Homer's *Odyssey*, the *Grail* legends, myths and fairy tales, men and women alike have ingested the archetypal "plot" for the male hero: his triumphant journey through tests and trials passed and overcome in his practice of the heroic virtues of courage, fortitude, and temperance. He is throughout life the agent of his own fate, secure in the knowledge that the gods help those who help themselves. His journey's home is the arms of the princess or the waiting, loving and weaving Penelope.

Later in the annals, toward the end of the eighteenth century, Jean-Jacques Rousseau invented a new archetype of male history with his romantic hero stressing the rights and place of sentiment in the life of man and celebrating the uniqueness of each individual. The specifically American addition to that scenario appeared with Benjamin Franklin's *Autobiography*, presenting the self-made man, rising from poverty to economic independence and public trust earned by his unfailing thrift, industry and moderation. This most beloved script among American males lives on in the writings by Horatio Alger and in the ever-popular biographies of enterprising males such as John Adams, Andrew Carnegie, Henry Ford, and Lee Iacocca.

With such models in their portfolios, no wonder most men experience a substantial loss of male identity at the termination of their careers; nor is it unreasonable to expect that extensive research would be expended on the topic.

Such is not the case for professional women whose primary identity until recently has been perceived as that of homemaker even as they walk out the door in the morning to join the workforce. The girls reading the same stories and fairy tales as the boys rarely saw a part for themselves other than that of waiting princess, despite the fact that Gretel fooled the witch by telling Hansel to substitute a twig for his finger as their nearsighted jailor demanded to test it through the bars as a gauge of body fat and suitability for dinner. Ariadne was abandoned on Naxos as Theseus sailed on to Athens even though she had furnished the thread that allowed him to find his way out of the labyrinth after slaying the Minotaur.

Except for Heidi who threw off her shoes and gave her cheese to Peter the shepherd so she might roam the alps without impediments, some of us found slim response to our quest for models in either classical or romantic literary tradition. The former gave the only women heroes, the Amazons, a bad reputation; the latter plotted an equally restrictive ending of either nunnery or marriage. We held out hopes for Cathy Earnshaw as she "wuthered" through her childhood and teen years with swarthy Heathcliff, but she married pale Edgar and died soon thereafter.

Even today it takes some searching to find a woman's story of her life that admits her own agency in it and *her happiness in effecting it.* We are grateful for Jill Conway's journey from Coorain to the presidency of Smith College and Katherine Graham's *Personal History* even as we realize they were prompted—and thus "legitimized"—by necessity: Conway's need to escape the grueling and culturally barren outback and Graham's sudden loss of her husband, which offered her the opportunity to decide the future of "her father's paper."

Nor has the movie industry done us any favors. A team of researchers, Markson and Taylor, at Boston University Gerontology Centre, found severe gender biases in the answer to their question: "Have changing demographics, increased life expectancy and findings about gender similarities and differences, altered portrayals of older people in American feature films during the past 65 years?" They investigated more than three thousand feature films made between 1929 and 1995 showing actors and actresses who were over sixty, and who had been nominated at least once in their lifetime for an Oscar. The result of their studies showed that "throughout this period, men were more likely [than women] to be depicted as vigorous, employed and involved in same-gender friendships and adventure (whether as hero or villain). Women remained either peripheral to the action or were portrayed as rich dowagers, wives/mothers, or lonely spinsters."

Despite changing gender roles in later life since the 1930's and despite social and economic changes for older Americans, their portrayals had remained noticeably static in age and gender stereotyping. In feature films, the mask of ageing, furthermore, differs by gender. "Male masks veil inactivity and physical changes, while female masks reveal ageist and sexist stereotypes." Actors may choose among the masks of "artful trickery and playfulness ... daring ... sincerity ... sinister manipulation ... authenticity"—whereas actresses "grow up and grow old—often to become tedious, timid or termagant." Those portrayals are potentially powerful. Explicitly and implicitly they may dictate and influence behaviors and attitudes and shape our values regarding age and gender roles.

We have furthermore learned that ingrained perceptions of social behaviors die hard. This was especially well illustrated during World War Two when women's hands and brains were recruited for their own as well as men's work, and yet their designation and reputation as wives, mothers and homemakers was left entirely intact. The returning men may have feared for their jobs, which had temporarily been filled by their wives, but only a few would perceive that a change in gender roles had occurred. Surely the war years had been an aberration, a break in a routine that would be reestablished as soon as families were re-united and brought back to "normal." The returning warrior had come home to find an independent woman where he had expected patient Penelope or ardent Cordelia whose voice, as her father King Lear reminds us, was "ever soft, gentle and low; an excellent thing in woman." We may all be in accord with Shakespeare on the excellence of that; yet few of us like to experience intensity and outward directed passion—celebrated in males as a key to upward mobility—construed as shrillness and unwifely behavior in females.

Our discomfort at the denigration of women's individual engagement in the world is reluctantly admitted by several of the women in *Facing the Mirror,* Frida Kerner Furman's anthropological study of a group of women in their sixth, seventh and eighth decades frequenting a neighborhood beauty parlor. Most women of their generation gave up work when they married to support the illusion that a man's job was to provide for his wife and family. Anna, however, who was married during the war, continued doing office-work while her husband was in the service. One day he came home. "I was working for a company and [my husband] came in; a cousin of mine was working there too, and he came in to say 'hello.' He came into my boss's office to say, 'This is your last day.' He never let me go back to work. The only fights we ever had were when I said, 'I am going to go to work,' because we certainly could have used the money, and he wouldn't let me go to work. It was a sore spot with him, and he wouldn't talk to me for a couple of days."

Yet male warriors turned peace workers gradually realized that times were changing. Increasingly American women would seek advanced college degrees and launch careers other than domestic. During those years, the 1960's, Betty Friedan's *The Feminine Mystique* helped some women initiate departure from the romantic myth, a separation which subsequently was fortified by contemporary poets and writers as well as rediscovered authors such as Virginia Woolf.

Virginia Woolf's continued influence on women's lives shows in the recent film success of *The Hours*. The film records the lives of three independent women: the writer Woolf, the mother, who, to survive with herself intact, leaves her husband and two young children, and the business woman who lives with her lesbian partner and plans a birthday party for a former male lover. The popularity of a film celebrating women's autonomy suggests a willingness on the part of moviegoers to consider alternative modes for living and to temper conventional judgment of the mother who leaves her two young children to preserve her identity, the writer who demands "a room or her own," and a woman who is both mother and lesbian.

On the part of its makers, *The Hours*, furthermore, shows a perceived change in occupational roles portrayed by women as mature and elderly females. Released in 2002, it features a writer, a librarian, and an editor. All three present a vivid contrast to the examples found in "The Mirror Has Two Faces," the Markson and Taylor study, which show that the most frequent "occupation" for women was being rich society matrons, followed by the category of spouses or parents not in the labor force. These classifications are non-existent among male roles, all of which were of "major professionals." Absence in *The Hours* of the earlier archetypal rich woman—laughable, domineering, interfering—or the oppressive widow or mother figure furthermore suggests that a change in depiction of mature or elderly women is occurring. The mother who leaves her two young children reappears at the end of the movie as a librarian who has made an authentic life for herself after breaking away from her family. With that outcome, her existential—and unconventional—choice to abandon her family is portrayed as redeemable.

"To a woman it does not seem odd to think of herself as a unique person," writes Dianne Johnson in a review of Andrew Hacker's *Mismatch: The Growing Gulf Between Men and Women*, "an individual with habits and attributes, and, as it happens, with the ability to bear children. Modern American women, at least, also have an expectation of a kind of autonomous moral and intellectual sentience independent of biology." This expectation of relatively recent origin is born of the knowledge that biology as destiny remains an unproven thesis. Nor has the scientific community as yet reached an agreement on the roles of nature and nurture in deciding female consciousness.

One stereotype seems to have remained largely unchanged: society's vision of old women as "left over," bereft of sexual appeal and function and suspect as full time nurturers moving in the direction of needing nurturing themselves. This "negative social response to different stages of the process of aging" Baba Copper labels ageism. In *Over the Hill: Reflections on Ageism Between Women* she distinguishes between aging as a biological process and ageism as a kind of "social aging ... Aging is a real process, which takes place differently in each individual. Ageism, on the other hand, is a constriction that rearranges power relationships, just like any other kind of discrimination or prejudice. When one ages, one may gain or lose. With ageism, one is shaped into something that is *always* less than what one really is." The ageism which old women experience, she continues, "is firmly embedded in sexism— an extension of the male power to define, control values, erase, disempower and divide. Woman-to-woman ageism is an aspect of the horizontal conflict which usurps the energies of the colonized—part of the female competition for the crumbs of social power."

Such general denigration of older women has, in Copper's opinion, been the historical norm since the days of witch-hunts when suspicion of witchcraft fell on any old woman with a wrinkled face. Freudian discourse continued this disparagement of the ageing body as a sign of deformation, "a narcissistic wound to the ego," especially to that of a woman, whose dysfunction is "written on her body in folds and wrinkles for everyone to see." The image that comes to mind of anyone who has seen the movie *Lost Horizons* is of the horror on the young soldier's face as he looks into the visage of his bride-to-be whom he has led across the mountains separating Shangri La from the real world. He is witnessing the transformation of a lovely young maid turned withering crone, and he recoils.

Freud is not alone in his disavowal of aged females. His colleague in medicine Doctor Nascher, who coined the term "geriatrics," opined that the lives of the aged are useless, a burden to themselves and to the community at large. He saw in the elderly "an old person" a gender-less personality made up of "masculine" traits such as nobility, virility and bravery and "female" characteristics like nurturance, domesticity and passivity.

No wonder some of us are reluctant to lay down the shield of professional practice and expertise, which wards off the ubiquitous effects of ageism as it signals our place and function in the world. Put in a different way, a professional woman will look in a mirror and see a woman in a suit, not an aging crone. Devoid of shield and suit, we risk being seen as less able than before, no longer deserving of "being heard," but available for utilization by others.

We mentioned earlier our ready acceptance of men's careers as signal and definition of their identity. That acceptance furthermore encompasses our acknowledgment of those careers as being in many cases sublimation endeavors: frustrated or troublesome personal relationships turned into market productivity. We have been somewhat slower to realize that the same is the case for many professional women who have turned to careers as a source of satisfaction in their lives as great or greater than the contentment they experience or experienced in their roles of wives, mothers, or both. Some entered their professions early on in their marriage; others only after their years of child rearing had run their course. In either case, many professional women have had a long struggle to attain their positions in a man's world, and their success has given them a great sense of satisfaction. It is therefore reasonable to assume that professional women on retirement may suffer equally weighty separation issues as those of men. That assumption puts up for debate the issue of whether it is actually easier for professional women to retire than for professional men because women may at any time return to perform their traditional roles as home makers and "natural" caregivers and thus suffer little separation anxiety or loss of professional identity. They, so the argument goes, never lost their primary identity as wives, mothers and grandmothers and thus have retained a guaranteed fallback position.

That this conventional wisdom may be off the mark, however, is suggested not only by women's acknowledgment of lost professional identity but by our perception of a certain dread, anxiety about the unknown, experienced and signaled by those who postpone their date with retirement. We spoke to a Los Angeles dentist in her seventies who practices with her husband. She would like to terminate a long and satisfactory career but can't quite take the plunge. Dread of herself-without-a-dental-career holds her back. Herself in that role, which is no role as she perceives it, is outside "the range of her imagination" and she hesitates to bring it inside "the range of experience."

This woman's dread reveals something other and more than discomfort at being a potential object of ageism, as well as acknowledgement of lost identity in terms of salary, social contacts, and intellectual stimulation. Something less easily defined and much less easily countermanded. It requires self evaluation at a level rarely exercised in the press of daily career activities which allow and even invite functioning on automatic pilot. The dynamics which prompt acknowledgment of ourselves, relationship with ourselves, and finally choosing ourselves as work in progress are rooted in emotions, knowledge and will, all of which must combine and fuel a passion which, in turn, may urge us toward exploration and commitment.

That is an exacting process, and many people—not only retiring professional women—dread the process and possibility of becoming real to themselves and therefore avoid it at all costs. The routine of career life aids such avoidance, and retirement life certainly permits it, as Tennessee Williams' scathing observations of the "overbusy" retired person Mrs. Stone would suggest. She pursues, he writes, "little diversions, the hairdresser at four o'clock, the photographer at 5:00, the Colony at 6:00, the theatre at 7:30, Sardi's at midnight ... she moved in the great empty circle. But she glanced inward from the periphery and saw the void enclosed there. She saw the emptiness ... but the way that centrifugal force prevents a whirling object from falling inward, she was moved for a long time from the void she circled." Mrs. Stone, he suggests, is busy but does not seem to know what she is busy about.

In a similar way, Norman Cousins speaks of "the centrifuge of the twentieth century," which has man "whirling away from the center of his own being" towards a separation "between body and place ... between mind and reason." This observation of man's increasing estrangement from himself despite more leisure hours and potential time for reflection makes him conclude that retirement "supposed to be a chance to join the winner's circle, has turned out to be more dangerous than automobiles or LSD." Retirement, he continues, is for many people "literal consignment to no-man's land ... the chance to do everything that leads to nothing ... the gleaming brass ring that unhorses the rider." Against such odds, Cousins warns us, we must gather all our powers to not only resist but prevail.

Finally, the void some of us experience as dread of being-oneself-without-a-vocation is furthered by our resistance to cross the threshold into the Third Stage. We are aware that the Reaper might have harvested us at any stage, but we know for a fact that we will meet Him there and, consequently, we find safety in postponement.

Given, then, the loss of professional identity in terms of salary, social contacts and intellectual stimulation, granted the general denigration of older women, and considering the dread vis a vis ourselves without our professions and under compunction to chart a new course, contemporary professional women are not likely to buy into the assumption that their anxiety on retiring is necessarily less than that experienced by their male counterparts because of a fall-back position of wives and homemakers.

It is true that for some women a shift from professional to resumed domestic identity—wife, mother, grandmother—may be desirable and satisfying *if the transformation is consciously made and willingly chosen.* But, that does not diminish the caveat sounded by professional women who fear that in giving up the identity a career confers, they will resume the status of "wife" in a twenty-four hour relationship with a husband who is always at home, of "mother" as a "babysitter-on-call," or as care givers for older relatives.

A comment from a retired professional of our acquaintance, "oh, I could grow geraniums in my kitchen sink" implicitly rejects those potential engagements. It trumpets a note of defiance and stakes a claim to the land of individual creativity that does not necessarily include domestic duty. Along that line, the Wingrove and Slevin report on women in the workplace notes that "not a single woman mentioned housework as a major activity or source of meaning in her life earlier or in retirement. Actually, most continue to have weekly domestic help, and many mentioned their dislike of household chores." Cooking was an exception. Among women in the study—even those who did not take it up until after retirement—many found making food "a form of creativity and a necessary adjunct of entertaining." Perceived as a gesture of personal satisfaction in contrast to a domestic chore, cooking might accommodate even May Sarton's insistence that women must become "persons first and wives second" and subtract nothing from the glee with which she reports that her younger women friends are developing in that direction.

That some older women may have moved along the same line is suggested by the fact that several studies conducted during the eighties and nineties show older men finding marriage more satisfying and experiencing fewer negative emotions about their marital lives than do older women. This alleged disconnect between older husbands' and older wives' perception of marriage in retirement may be explained by the formers' readiness to engage on the home front after a long career span, whereas their wives may have started later in their careers and lack the readiness to resume domestic duties. Thus some men may be seen as moving toward home and hearth activities and some women as moving away.

Current research investigating marital satisfaction has found the effects of retirement on spousal relations both positive and negative. Some couples report increasingly satisfying companionship and a more relaxed home atmosphere with more time to do things together and talk about plans and experiences. Others reveal that too much time spent together has resulted in mutual irritation. The wife experienced her husband "underfoot," and he was made to feel he should seek ways of avoiding being there, which put a strain on his social skills at a time when he was counting on his wife to provide their social engagements and activities.

That the opposite response may also be the case is demonstrated in a *New York Times* article from March 2004 titled "He's Retired, She's Working, They're Not Happy." Laura Radin in New Jersey "looked forward to following her husband, Rodney Lemberger, into retirement. 'I had my own ideas of what would happen,' she said. 'I'd spend time with my husband, take care of things around the house, travel. I found out I was invading his space. He had already carved out his life during the day time.'" The four years separating their retirement dates had allowed Mr. Lemberger to develop his own interests, and he was not prepared to go "here and there together," as his wife had envisioned them doing during her pre-retirement "planning."

The Radin/Lemberger experience might suggest that staggered retirement is less desirable than retirement in tandem. That, indeed, the article alleges is what "most couples say." And yet, "in 2000 there were more than two million couples in which a man 55 or over had not worked in the previous year, but his wife had. These accounted for 19.9 percent of couples involving a man 55 or over, up from 1.6 million such couples, or 9.6 percent of the total, in 1990."

"This mismatch does not work very well," opines Phyllis Moen, a sociologist at the University of Minnesota. She also points out we are the first generation to deal with what she labels an "altered marital dynamic of retirements," which leaves us with no models or blueprints from prior generations who by and large experienced only one retirement, that of the man in the house. Retirement, we may agree, has become a complicated issue as an article in *Journal of Family Issues* from May, 2004 puts it, " Effects of the retirement transitions [on marriage] are far subtler than previously believed."

Even at that, transitions may have in them a seed of positive change as Laura Schultz's Letter to the Editor regarding "He's Retired, She's Working ..." would suggest: "Boomer women are a huge group of capable, healthy and self-assured women who are redefining what it means to be a woman at midlife and beyond. Retirement and marriage will never be the same again!"

A similarly positive note rings out from a recent "My Word" column in *AARP*, "Taking the Plunge." Richard Atcheson is literally taking the plunge in an aerobics class with "eight white-haired ladies bobbing in the water" and figuratively in the kitchen "trying to figure things out." With trial and error, fixing and eating a lot of scrambled eggs till he got them right, he now invites people to brunch "with total aplomb." He can "squeeze a grapefruit and thump a melon," even host a lunch or dinner on the supposition that "with the years, we all have to get used to new learning and curious developments."

Obviously individual features of temperament and inclinations make a difference. The retired professional woman who chooses a new or renewed career as wife, mother, grandmother, home maker/ care giver consciously embraces—or willingly submits to—an identity she never lost entirely even as it may for a time have been superseded by that of teacher, physician or CEO. In her retirement, she may resume her initial and perhaps most strongly imprinted identity and play it out in all the facets of "home" activities.

A case in point is our friend Jeanette who retired with her husband when they sold the winery they had jointly owned and managed. They eventually moved to another part of the state and bought a house there which for a while claimed their full attention. That put in order, Jeanette took up quilting on a more or less full time basis. Taking classes and going to workshops involved her in the new community, and with increasing expertise she began showing and occasionally selling her work. Eventually quilting yielded to beading, which may down the line be succeeded by other activities. Yet because Jeanette's identity is grounded in that of wife and mother, she has an inexhaustible source from which to draw, as people and relationships are always works in progress, especially if they become one's total or primary agenda.

Hobbies and activities are for Jeanette given significance by her husband's active or passive participation and interest, but she is not expecting her engagements to give her a life or to be her life's work—her husband is. She will not be disappointed as one by one her involvements may lose their attraction, unlike some women who have looked forward to spending more time in workshops, on the tennis court, playing bridge, or taking sewing classes only to learn that those engagements do not provide the work they crave.

Women who feel that hobbies and activities are not enough to sustain a life may not love or value their husbands any less than do those for whom their mates lend meaning and significance to all their actions. It is just that the former have different expectations for themselves. Freed of bosses or supervisors and released from what is traditionally called the "work place," they want nonetheless to have work to do, self assigned and self generated, work which demands commitment of time and attention, work which will give them reason for being and from which they will never "retire." They will work hard, but because their rewards are intrinsic to the task, it will be close to play.

Our readings on the topic have repeatedly supported this contention and made the claim that many professional women desire to continue work in their Third Stage, *no matter what their financial circumstances may be.* Such work may be a continuation of the profession they practiced in their employment years, something tangential, or something entirely different.

Some women sign on part time with their former employers or new employers, or they use their skills and knowledge to start up their own businesses, which may be similar or different from work they did before retirement. Some volunteer for political or social causes they feel passionate about. To earn the "work" designation, post retirement pursuits need not be remunerative in terms of money. For satisfaction and a key to the good life, however, they must be challenging. Their hallmark is engagement and focused attention.

Writer and retired university professor Carolyn Heilbrun made commitment to work the cornerstone of her retirement house as she explains in *The Last Gift of Time*, and Betty Friedan echoes her choice. "Thinking about the groups that live longest in our society," Friedan alleges, "one senses the following: they are all involved in work that keeps them developing and using their abilities to the fullest. And their work demands and uses the qualities that emerge in age—the ability to see the picture whole, and its meaning deep, and tell it true: wisdom. And it is real work that is needed and for which they are respected. They do not have to pretend to be young. They are not expected to decline in age in the qualities for which they are valued—and they do not."

Heilbrun and Friedan speak of creative projects which are self-started, self-sponsored and inexhaustible; one generates another. Independent of institutions or companies, they are the work of free women in precisely the way Edith Hamilton speaks of the ancient Greeks' capacity for happiness rooted in their "exercise of vital powers along lines of excellence in a life affording them scope." Acknowledging "scope" in terms of abundant options, she does not address the nature of such "exercise," only the craft in carrying it out, engagement and commitment, and the role of environment for its pursuit.

However wide or narrow is the range of options our society affords, we do at this time in our lives have some control over our environment, geographically or metaphorically. No longer tethered to Columbia University, Carolyn Heilbrun bought herself a retirement house where she could write her books. She made a geographical move. We, too, may have a choice about staying where we are, or moving to a different place more conducive to leading the good life all of us would welcome for the remains of our days, or we may learn that environment is determined to some extent by the lenses we craft for seeing it.

All of us will grant its importance, and some, like Isak Dinesen, would contend that a woman's environment is crucial to her well being. *Out of Africa* is her testament to that conviction. It is a tribute to her affection for the African countryside and its natives as a "magnificent enlargement" of her world, which in *Shadows on the Grass* she credits with increasing the resonance of her voice with echoes of melodies heard all around her. Twenty-two years, 1937-60, separate the two works, but her initial feeling of waking up in the African highlands in 1913 with the knowledge "here I am where I ought to be" never lost its savor. For a time, she had placed herself where she felt most alive, and when the double bankruptcy of marriage and coffee plantation forced her to leave, she bemoaned not her forfeited roles of wife and manager, but the loss of echoes in her new/old environment and the resourceful interplay of individual and world.

Back in the house where she grew up, in the environment not of her choosing, she slowly and painfully committed herself to a career as a teller of stories and was rewarded with the truth that had caught up with fellow writer Eudora Welty, that the " open mind and the receptive heart—which are at last with fortune's smile the informed mind and the experienced heart—are to be gained anywhere, any time, without necessarily moving an inch from any present address. Surely" she writes, "there are as many ways of seeing a place as there are eyes to see it. The impact happens in so many different ways."

With her stories Dinesen wrote herself into the world from where she had set out. So, too, must we in the environment which frames our lives in the Third Stage, wherever we are, write our stories—in becoming ourselves—by whatever means we can.

As our use of first person plural would suggest, we are—even as we write—at work to live the lives we advocate, the life we consider good. The good life has in it as many dimensions as we care to perceive and explore. So far, we have made it appear that the *examined* life we posit as a basis for the *good* life is one that mostly the mind can procure, but as Shakespeare teaches us with

Coriolanus, our stomachs must be accorded equal importance and function.

Addressing the citizens of Rome, who complain that the Senate cram their own storehouses and "suffer [them] to famish," Coriolanus's friend Menenius likens them to body parts rebelling against their bellies for being "idle and unactive," unseeing, unhearing, "undevising and uninstructive." Not so, answers the belly. "True it is, ... That I receive the general food at first/Which you do live upon; and fit it is/Because I am the store house and the shop of the whole body. But if you do remember/I send it through the rivers of your blood,/Even to the court, the heart, to th' seat o' th' brain/And, through the cranks and offices of man/The strongest nerves and small inferior veins /From me receive that natural competency by which they live." Considering that our "natural competency," that is, sufficient fuel for each body part to function, depends on our stomachs, we may be well advised by English lexicographer Dr. Johnson's belief that "he who does not mind his belly will hardly mind anything else."

Advocates of "the good life" abound, but we are fortunate to have learned from a master: Angelo Pellegrini. He taught Shakespeare for many years at the University of Washington, a vocation he loved but no more than he did his avocation: cooking fresh, well prepared food using home grown vegetables and berries and serving it to friends with generous pourings of self made wines. That recipe for the good life he had brought with him from his childhood mountain village in Tuscany. As a professor and a chef, he would speak of a "sane, wholesome attitude toward food and drink" as a basic principle in living the good life.

This enthusiasm for good food and the respect we owe it, Pelle shared with us on two occasions when he and his wife, Virginia, came to stay at Inga's house after signing books in a friend's kitchen store. It was in the early eighties and *The Foodlover's Garden* had just been published. Fresh food is abundant in Yakima, and came dinnertime, Pelle "fell to," as he put it, in the kitchen. He taught us to start our breads with a biga and to cook chicken the Italian way with olive oil, vermouth, parsley, onions, rosemary, garlic and lemon. The hastily scribbled notes on a card in our recipe box suggests that we learned as he went along. Watching those deft hands rubbing and herbing the chicken and listening to his basso profundo explaining the process and inviting our participation were wonderful kitchen adventure. The hour and a half or so the bird roasted in the oven, we spent in quiet anticipation of the emerging meal, making salad, sipping wine, quoting Shakespeare, and talking about Tuscany and Florence where it turned out we had stayed at the same Pensione. As smells of herbs and chicken drifted out through the open door to the porch where we sat, we savored the evening, luxuriating in time spent in such satisfying company. Dinner surpassed expectations, and we enjoyed it "with gratitude and thanksgiving," in respect for the growth of the soil and the hands that brought it to the table. No wonder that man had "troops of friends" till the day he died. Even a losing battle with prostate cancer spared him Macbeth's bitter realization that "the wine of life is drawn, and the mere lees is left this vault to brag of." Pelle's world never saw the lees; it had plenty of wine left over.

Pellegrini was unimpressed with the quality of cookery books on the market in the forties and thought the American housewife who "would venture beyond the limited orbit of tinned foods and watery roasts" badly misled. He would, however, have applauded the women in the Wingrove and Slevin study who thought cooking a creative undertaking and have encouraged the retired men who come around to thinking that cooking might be considered a worthwhile learning experience in a field demanding everyone's engagement at some level. As his memoir/cookbook, *The Unprejudiced Palate,* shows, Pelle thought cooking worth engagement at all levels, from growing the food, preparing and cooking it, to eating it with friends and conversations in summer gardens and winter dining rooms.

Throughout these years we have followed where he led, steadily minding our bellies. With this text we will make no exception. Making enjoyable virtue of acknowledged necessity to feed, we will savor food's variations and endless possibilities and invite everyone's participation. The recipe suggestions here are the result of shared food ventures through forty years of dinners, running like a red thread through the tapestry of friendship.

Eating and cooking are, for us, closely aligned with the changing seasons, which where we live dictate the growing of fresh fruits and vegetables. We like especially the hopes and promises of spring, so this virtual invitation is to join our habitual greeting of the vernal equinox with the first halibut of the year.

Halibut—Marinated and Barbequed

Buy a thick slice of halibut, enough to satisfy four good eaters.

Marinade:
½ cup of soy sauce
1 cup dry white wine
2 T. lemon juice
2 cloves garlic, minced
1 tsp. powdered ginger
½ cup salad oil
Have on hand:
2 T. fresh rosemary
6 T. chopped parsley

Pour marinade over fish and let sit for four hours or for however much time you have. Pour off marinade and save. Sprinkle fish with 2 T. fresh rosemary and about 6 T. fresh chopped parsley. Place on grill over low coals using foil for a base or placing fish in wire broiler. Cook until fish flakes easily when tested with a fork, about 10 to 15 minutes, basting occasionally with part of the marinade

To complement the delicate flavor of the year's first catch, we may serve a creamy risotto with sprinkled-on chives which we cook as our husbands grill the fish and pour the first glasses of wine. We like the youngest available Sauvignon Blanc from New Zealand, a local Fume Blanc or perhaps an Italian Pinot Grigio. They are in-your-face wines that will sing out in accompanying the first bites of halibut. We will on occasion let the salad course move us to trying a young, somewhat fruity red wine like the Italian Sangioviese, which is now produced locally as well, or a California Gamay or Syrah. Vinegar makes salads and wines uneasy partners, but we nonetheless enjoy their relationship.

Creamy Risotto with Chives

4 T. olive oil
1 cup onion, finely chopped
2 cups Arborio rice
1 cup dry white wine
6 cups chicken broth
Chives

Heat oil and sauté onion till softened. Add rice and stir. Add wine and cook till absorbed. Add just enough chicken broth to cover the rice. Cook, uncovered, stirring constantly until broth is absorbed. Continue this process till all broth has been absorbed. It will take about 15 minutes. Served with chopped chives.

We serve salad as a second course—easier on both the hostess and the wine—and with this dinner we often have a lusty spinach and avocado combination, which adds a fruity flavor to the gentle tastes of fish and rice. "Green is good for the eyes," said Hans Christian Andersen, and the succulent sheen and vivid color of the spinach present a pleasing contrast to the predominantly white appearance of the main course.

Spinach and Avocado Salad

10 oz. spinach leaves
1 ripe avocado
2 T. lemon juice
½ English cucumber, peeled and sliced
Dressing:
3 T. balsamic vinegar
1 T. honey
1 clove garlic, minced

½ tsp. salt and 3 T. olive oil
2 T. toasted chopped walnuts

Toast nuts at 350 till lightly brown—10-15 minutes. Place spinach in a bowl. Peel avocado and slice. Toss avocado with lemon juice and arrange on spinach. Add cucumber slices. In a small bowl, whisk vinegar and honey, garlic and salt. Whisk in olive oil. Toss with salad and sprinkle with nuts.

We will finish with Alice's Layer Cake, a recipe from the old country made by Alice on festive occasions and now serving a second and third generation of well-pleased palates. Alice is gone now, but as we eat our version of her concoction, we celebrate the old and nourish the new as we hold her in our hearts' and minds' embrace.

Alice's Layer Cake

¼ cup butter
½ cup sugar
4 egg yolks, beaten
1 cup flour
2 tsp. baking powder
½ cup milk

Cream butter and sugar. Add the remaining ingredients, alternating powders and liquids. Spoon into two 9-inch pans.

Meringue:
4 egg whites
¼ cup sugar
½ tsp. vanilla

A generous handful of blanched almonds or walnuts Beat whites till stiff. Add sugar gradually. Spread evenly on top of batter in the two pans. Sprinkle on almonds or walnuts. Bake at 360 for approximately 15-20 minutes.

Custard Filling:
Make the simplest custard we know, requiring no double boiler, just vigorous stirring.
4 T. flour
1 T. cornstarch
1/3 cup sugar
Pinch of salt
2 cups milk
2 eggs
1 T. vanilla
1 dab of butter
½ cup whipping cream

Add first four ingredients to saucepan. Turn heat to medium and stir till bubbles form. Beat the two eggs and add to mixture. Keep stirring and cooking till more bubbles form. Remove from heat and add vanilla and butter. Cool. Whip the cream and add to custard, a little at a time. Spread custard between the two cooled cake layers. Serve and enjoy.

Our combination of food on this occasion reminds us that whether we wish it or not, time marches forward. Seasons and people are transient. We cannot go back to where we were, but we can retain the skills we gained and continue to explore in an effort to establish a continuity of selves along our life spans. Alfred Lord Tennyson, one of the eminent Victorians, shows us the way in his poem about Ulysses returning to Ithaca from the battlefields of Troy. It is a poem of homecoming. Some ten years it has taken him to arrive, and he may well have had it in him to wish for a time to rest and farm his lands. But his explorer's mind would not let him move back to where he had been, would not let him "profit" as an "idle king," so he rouses his men and sets out for other shores relying on his sailor's skills for navigation: "Tho' much is taken, much abides; and tho'/We are not now that strength which in old days/Moved earth and heaven; that which we are, we are ... strong in will/To strive, to seek, to find, and not to yield." Once drafted to set sail for Troy, Ulysses was now on a self appointed voyage and did not shirk the challenge. He had learned the motions of going out and coming back, seeking adventure and returning home, and in the process building a life.

Similarly, we should not deprive ourselves of a life story or think we have reached the angle of repose merely because we have put a period to our career narratives. As we pussy foot around the realization that the market place will suffer no reduction by our absence, we would be wise to convince ourselves that we still have work to do, texts to write with our lives. If we accept Marya Schechtman's argument in *The Construction of Selves* that we create our identity by shaping an autobiographical narrative—writing it or living reflectively—then we must go on weaving, as it were, the fabric of our lives that shows us who we are. We must absorb our career identities into our larger, more encompassing mental and spiritual framework, fit Ulysses' explorations into the tapestry of Penelope's weaving.

Others have arrived at the same conclusion. In their Introduction to *Women Confronting Retirement*, Nan Bauer-Maglin and Alice Radosh quote the findings of an Australian study of older professional women noting that "Retirement no longer means the withdrawal from active engagement in the workforce, to a life of leisure, but a readjustment, a finer balance of time and energy to allow a more creative and satisfying engagement with the many sides of life and self.

This balance is unlikely to be found either in narrowly defined full-time paid work or in the absence of paid employment. Women are looking for a balance of socially useful work, meaningful social relations with friends and family, the opportunity to explore and develop new creative energies, and time for themselves. Such a balance may be found in full-time employment or in retirement, but is more likely to require something in-between. For all the above reasons, older women of this cohort are disinclined to think or talk in terms of retirement, but are seeking new creative forms of living."

Are we an arrogant lot? Perhaps. Yet we insist that moving toward death is not the same thing as treading a dead end, and we will go on encouraging exploration of possibilities for leading the good life.

2

FROM SALARIES TO COINS OF TIME

I am a part of all that I have met;
Yet all experience is an arch wheretrho'
Gleams that untravell'd world, whose margin fades
For ever and for ever when I move.
How dull it is to pause, to make an end, ...
Little remains: but every hour is saved
From that eternal silence, ...
And this gray spirit yearning in desire
To follow knowledge like a sinking star,
Beyond the utmost bound of human thought.

— Alfred Lord Tennyson, "Ulysses."

Whatever the size of our income, in our career worlds we generated cash for practicing our professions and spending our life hours. Some of us had to make a living; others wanted money to build the life we wanted for ourselves and our families, and everyone was rewarded by the status and independence money accords in a culture that by and large values work by the compensation it fetches. No matter our incentives, retirement makes equals of us all in the sense that now we trade income for time, a much more illusive coin which like all earnings may be frittered away or wisely spent.

Throughout our employment lives, personal time gave way to hours dedicated to professional tasks and domestic demands. In our ambivalence toward that allotment, we may have sighed with Andrew Marvell, "Had we but world enough and time," and at the same time lamented with Wordsworth that "the world is too much with us/late and soon getting and spending ... " To our surprise, perhaps, we may find that in retirement life—at least at first—we may have time enough, but the "world" is no longer with us. Certainly not, if with that designation we understand the career world of which we were a part, but which no longer provides a designated place for our endeavors and no longer depends for anything on our contribution. The world may never really have known such dependence; yet that is what most of us like to think as we practice our skills and disseminate our knowledge.

Unlike our employment world, retirement land has neither boundaries nor charted space. We must not only map it but design roles for ourselves as individual inhabitants, a potentially greater challenge than any we encountered in our professional lives. To hold up the day, each day, without the props of functions and routines carried out in designated worlds inhabited by superiors, peers, and clients in one form or another, not only demands self generated energy but provides an extravagant opportunity for failure.

Time for catching on is limited. We may experience a feeling of more time in each twenty-four hour day; yet we are simultaneously aware that we are given much less time to waste than ever before. Young people are not inclined to think they will die. They feel like Jane Eyre who, when asked how she might avoid the fires of Hell, answered, "I must try to stay well, Sir." So must we, but in retirement land we live with full awareness of time running out of scope and all we can do is let each moment sink deeply into our beings in a process of learning to live each day as if we were going to die.

As the pendulum between birth and death swings in increasingly shorter intervals, we must somehow learn to hear the beats as opportunities—not deadlines—and come to recognize that the swings have no fewer vibrations. What we lose in strength and agility, we gain in tolerance for ambiguity; and time is on our side. Not in scale or extension, but in depth: an abyss gaping in our faces or a treasure hold of experiences awaiting our exploration.

Our culture promotes a stretching of our life spans as far as they will go with luck, prudence and genetic dispositions, and most of us buy into that. Yet if we think about it, longevity genes as a variable need not play into a resolve to deepen the moments. To that opportunity we all have equal access, and given a retirement life that does not demand our taking on jobs to provide subsistence, we can devote some attention to practice being really present. Without being "double scheduled" and "multi tasked," we can learn to give each moment its full worth and register of response. That is our boon and our challenge.

Given room for rumination, we can note the hours of the day with which we may have been out of tune due to schedules requiring our presence during certain times. In retirement land we no longer have to get up in the dark. Like Noah in his Ark, we can watch through our bedroom windows the lightening sky turn red before sunrise or brighten to silvery gray on a rainy or foggy day. We may also observe the progressive northwards journey of the sun in late winter as it inches back the darkness of night to arrive at the vernal equinox. Autumn's equinox, in turn, will remind us that the years of our participation in the earth's circumnavigation of the sun are numbered in ever fewer ciphers, but we may practice hoping that when the last one comes, we have observed enough rounds to accept our place in the cycles and draw comfort from their rhythm.

"The readiness is all," says Hamlet to Horatio before his duel with Laertes which will end their lives at the touch of the poisoned foils. His final words, "The rest is silence," echo his realization, which we, too, may arrive at, that preparing ourselves to be courageous at the end is as much as we can bring to the event, no matter what lies beyond in terms of resurrection or annihilation.

It takes time to tune in to nature and perceive our place in it, for we are unaccustomed to listen and unused to being really present in the moment. Likely we have not granted each phase of our lives its fully plummeted due and attention. Prompted by time constraints, we have hurried from decade to decade. Now we need to push the river no longer because gradually the truth catches up with us that it flows by itself. Our task now is to connect "the passion and the prose" of our lives as E.M Forster shows in *Howard's End* with the marriage of high spirited Margaret Schlegel and business magnate Henry Wilcox. Find something you can be passionate about and lend it attention and commitment, he advises.

If we accept the changes that must occur and face the losses we experience as we move from employment status to retirement void and yet have not made plans for our lives, we may spend some time looking about for challenging pursuits. Yet spending time on 'looking about' or on seemingly unproductive ventures is not likely to be in our book of habits. "I always forget how important the empty days are, comments May Sarton, "how important it may be not to produce anything, even a few lines in a journal ... A day where one has not pushed oneself to the limit seems a damaged damaging day, a sinful day. Not so."

Giving ourselves time to contemplate options before acting on them may be time well spent even though our explorations may take us down blind alleys, and persistence will take courage and enterprise. Spencer Johnson's *Who Moved My Cheese* became a bestseller on that platform. Change happens, he asserts, and we must learn to cope. The curious, explorative mice of his fable adapt to change, run into dead ends but move on and eventually locate the new cheese places, unlike the littlepeople who refuse to acknowledge the disappearance of their accustomed and comfortable supplies and venture into the maze only as starvation becomes their harsh alternative.

We can't cling to the careers we used to pursue. At best, we can hedge our bets and for a while resume our accustomed employ on a part-time basis or as volunteers in our fields. Either option yields remuneration in the coins of satisfaction earned by helping individuals and community and in time left over for ourselves. Continuance in jobs we know and like to perform aids the maintenance of our prized professional identity in terms of income for some and social contacts and intellectual stimulation for all. It even buys us some leisure time and thus provides, it would seem, the best of all worlds. Yet, that arrangement, too, will eventually come to an end for one reason or another, and once again identity issues must be faced and dealt with.

Gail, who retired some twenty years ago as a public relations executive, has arrived at that realization. With a degree in journalism, she has over the years found several satisfactory outlets for her creativity in salaried or volunteered activities. She served as a consultant for businesses wanting to improve public relations, and for several years she was a cherished and respected newsletter writer for a community group promoting conservancy of a local canyon. An observant hiker and writer, Gail appreciated the canyon's spectacular geological formations and the home it provided for wildflowers and grasses from snow melt till flames of cottonwood and sumac along the creek that flows through it. She found great satisfaction in voicing her experiences there, articulating conservation issues, and inviting readers to seek out the canyon by themselves or on Earth Day when a professional geologist leads tours for anyone interested.

After ten years, Gail regretfully resigned from the newsletter job on the grounds that her computer skills had not kept up with the times and the process by which she produced copy could be more effectively handled by someone more adept at computer language. Gail is resourceful, and she will survive the loss of her career as well as subsequent volunteer tasks because well into her eighties, she still finds wonders in small things, such as making angels in the snow and leading hikes in the Canyon. Her story, however, reminds us all that we must choose to participate or not in the technological advances of the day and guide our choice by the work we aim to do and its dependence on those.

Roberta's story is of a professor who returned to work on a part-time basis. The pay was modest, but as a math teacher of many years, she would not be too burdened with homework and she would be excused from department meetings and committee work. Ironically, the freedom from those responsibilities became the shackles on her sense of worth. Teaching two math classes a quarter, she filled a temporary need of the college as a valued and workable tool in its day to day machinery, but relinquishing her vote in departmental and curricular decisions, she had sacrificed her place at the turning of the crank. Roberta decided to resign and look elsewhere for pursuits that would provide greater satisfaction.

Both Gail and Roberta, one mostly a volunteer and the other a paid employee, did part-time work in their professional fields and received great to moderate satisfaction as long as it lasted. But both jobs did come to an end, albeit for different reasons, and, once again, they faced the task of building authentic lives for themselves in one way or another.

Carolyn's choice of volunteer work takes a somewhat different direction, which may prove to have in it a longer perspective than either Gail's or Roberta's pursuits. A retired attorney and long time Rotarian, she accepts challenging Rotary assignments such as planning cable TV and Internet Foundation Seminars and depends on her legal expertise and past Rotary experience to carry them out. The work she undertakes will change over time, but her professional status and the respect it engenders will remain the same. Unlike Roberta, she has not placed herself among former full-time colleagues and therefore does not have to compare her contributions to theirs, and unlike Gail, she has remained computer literate. The same may be said for Betty Jane, a counselor, who, in response to our questionnaire, reported that she remains actively engaged in The League of Women Voters, an involvement which will demand staying up to date on changes in the political arena and will offer changing and challenging assignments. Tangential to Carolyn's experience are stories of people who like Wendy Wank go back to school to earn the credentials that separate volunteers from professionals in a given field. Wendy was a documentary film editor who volunteered at a Zen hospice in San Francisco, whereupon she decided to become a general nurse practitioner with a minor in HIV. "What made me interested in both these courses was my volunteering work. But when I was a volunteer, I didn't know anything about the medical stuff. Now, as a nurse, I am the person they talk to, who makes sure they get pain or comfort medication." The gist of the New York Times article featuring Wendy's story is a call for attention to "accelerated nursing programs," which have made it quicker for mature caregivers to become trained medical workers. That these programs are successful is indicated by their having "nearly tripled" since 1990.

Like Wendy Wank, film editor turned nurse, Jackie Iversen learned that meaningful tasks and respect for the volunteer carrying them out may not be corollaries of volunteer work *unrelated* to professional expertise. A businesswoman and CEO in an agricultural consulting firm, Jackie felt strongly about "giving something back" to a community which had been generous to her. On retiring, she therefore volunteered her services in a local senior center where she thought her managerial skills and business acumen might be of help. Assigned the job of stuffing envelopes three days in a row, she deemed that a waste of time, however, and instead volunteered her skills at a phone service designed to help potential students get acquainted with programs and enrollment procedures at the town's community college. Another round of envelopes for licking and stamping made Jackie realize that to volunteer in a meaningful way she would have to be a good deal more specific about what she volunteered for, to make sure the assigned tasks would make use of her talents and skills.

Jackie's experience resonates among the respondents in the group of retired professional women interviewed by Christine Ann Price for her study on *Women and Retirement: The Unexplored Transition*. An example is Ruth, who was a former editor and writer of several professional publications. She volunteered to "design and produce" a brochure for a local senior education program. "So we got together and designed a brochure which was promptly thrown away. I objected strenuously to it ... so I made all these comments, they threw all my comments away and I felt as though, you know, why am I spending my time doing something? ... and when I mentioned it, this is what I was told: 'We couldn't possibly let volunteers produce a brochure, ah, the staff people have to be responsible so we couldn't possibly turn something as important as that over to the ... volunteers.'"

Another woman in the same group found her competence questioned when a new faculty member who did not know her stepped in to introduce a speaker at a professional conference, a task that had been allocated Myrtle ... "you are feeling at that moment that you are viewed as someone who does not quite have the capability that you know you have ... You have had, ah, a very clearly defined role in which you were an administrator, you were an instructor, you were in business or you were wherever. All right, that was yesterday, today you are retired. No longer of that same status."

As examples of experiences demonstrating a lack of respect for the work of volunteers, Price furthermore labels them instances of social stereotypes based on "misconception of individual abilities." This stereotype of incompetent retiree or volunteer, she continues, is a subtle or not so subtle "display of ageism" which is inseparable from retirement status because most retirees are elderly and "considering the negative portrayal of older women in the media, it seems plausible that female retirees may be more likely to be stereotyped as unqualified and inexperienced than males." Again we are made to realize the onus on all of us who are "mature," and perhaps we get a glimmering sense of responsibility for finding ways to lift that burden from the shoulders of our younger professional sisters as they follow in our retirement footsteps.

That so many retired professional women, despite the mentioned caveats, seek part-time career engagements and volunteer activities may be partly explained by their providing a "world" in which to work and feel useful, a world which lends structure to the day and minimizes the efforts we must otherwise make to orchestrate our time. Nor are those expectations unrealistic as demonstrated by the numerous success stories told by contented volunteers, especially those who have worked to benefit children. Examples abound in retirement literature, and the recent "road map to retirement" *2 Young 2 Retire* devotes a full chapter to such stories interspersed with lists of "top volunteer opportunities" and reasons we should sign up. The authors, Howard and Marika Stone, make a strong case for engagement in that parade and offer good advice.

Yet another "world," which will allow an already established identity to function and flourish exists for those of us who have a family. We may reassume in a more full-time capacity the selves we maintained outside our professional lives as wives, mothers and grandmothers. Those of us, who have that option and perceive it as good, may choose to play those roles on a grander scale. Our newly won flexibility in terms of time may enable us to deepen our friendship with our adult children—on their time schedules—even as it may demand a certain subjugation of our egos to accept the fact that busy adult children, men and women alike, may not have as much time for us and our interests as we might wish. They feel the time pressures of their professions and are unaware of the different kinds of deadlines, potential strokes, failing hearts, or dementia, that in later years may so emphatically shackle our enterprise. Like all unpleasant facts, those eventualities are not likely to be internalized by any of us until we watch their occurrence among our peers.

We cannot, therefore, expect our children to consider our schedules as we must consider theirs because we alone know both sets of time lines and realize that it is rarely given two generations to achieve a similar understanding of the world in tandem. To be fair to those we take for granted was always a difficult proposition. We were busy, too, when our children were young and probably did not give them as much time then as they would have thought their due.

Ellie remembers a conversation with her then twelve year old Heidi as they passed a sign in front of a church encouraging parents to give their children their most precious gift: time. Heidi piped up from the back seat. "That is exactly what I want, mother, more of your time." A precocious child, Heidi had expressed what a great many children feel but are less apt to articulate.

Time allotments, who gives whom how much time, also enters into the relationship with grandchildren, especially if grandparents do not live next door. When they come visiting from other towns or states, grandparents, from the standpoint of children, will inevitably siphon away some time from their parents, which they thought rightfully belonged to them. Children of their generation are accustomed to being "watched" as they play or turn out for sports. They expect parent-audience applause to cheer them on. A relatively short visit, such as a week-end, may therefore lead to frustration for all three generations, as none of the adults can quite give or get enough attention to fill their or the children's needs.

As a case in point, Ellie's daughter Kathleen recently reported after a week-end visit of grandparents that her son Stuart had observed "they did not pay any attention to me, only to Hilary" [his sister] even though granddad had pitched numerous games before sitting down to a glass of wine with his daughter, and Stuart's aunt had played endless rounds of basketball, one on one.

That strain is somewhat relaxed during longer visits, which yield more time for everyone and settle into a daily rhythm. Kathleen's sister Mary, for example, will always have a love of gardening instilled by her farmer grandfather who on long summer visits to the Northwest would help her plant a garden and tend it. Over the winter, he would send her seeds, which together they would sow and water, and eventually Mary would return the favor with seeds reclaimed from her flowers and squashes. He planted a legacy, and she nurtures it.

The tension which lurks in most intergenerational gatherings is wonderfully released or entirely absent when the middle generation, the children's parents, leave for either a couple of days or a week. Children and grandparents can then devote all their available time to one another for reading stories, building tee-pees, or attending games or other performances. The added responsibility of young lives during a stay like that is well rewarded by the growing closeness between grandchildren and grandparents, fostered by the opportunity for grandparents to lay down their own tasks for a while and be really present in the world of their grandchildren. That is a welcome option we did not have in our career lives of heavy schedules.

A friend of ours tells of a wonderful ten days she spent caring for her two grandchildren, Peter and Frannie, just before school was out for the summer. Nine-year-old Peter liked to get up and get ready for school at his own pace, but five year old Frannie would come running into grandmother's bed every morning carrying her child's version of the Old and New Testament. Not a member of a church going family, but a compassionate little soul, she had got stuck on the information that people had killed Jesus and that was very sad. Talking about it did not alleviate her distress, so the two agreed to read through both Testaments and approach the story from the beginning.

Together they learned about God's preference of Abel for Kain, Samson the kamikaze temple destroyer, Jericho's trumpet, the birth of Christ, His miracles and finally His triumphant death as sacrifice and savior of all, including Frannie. She listened attentively to the stories as read to her—two times over—and nodded at her salvation in the scheme of things. But then she added, "It is still sad that they killed Jesus." It may sound as if no ground were gained—and yet—as a first lesson in the tolerance of ambiguity, it may stand Frannie in good stead as practice for the next. It is certain that her grandmother will never forget those early summer mornings contained by child and adult absorbed in the riches of the eternal story.

That such prolonged care-taking visits may sometimes founder on the bedrock of differing expectations, however, comes as no surprise. Each generation cherishes its own principles of child rearing, and sometimes grandparents think it their duty to impose some discipline where little or none is perceived to exist. Helen, who wrote from Vermont where she was taking care of two grandchildren while their parents were enjoying a hard earned week's vacation, reported overhearing the following conversation between the children, six and ten. "Do you want to hear some good news? She is leaving tomorrow." Helen's sense of humor stood her in good stead in the reporting, but her story nonetheless makes us question the extent to which we should attempt to impose our standards of behavior on our children's children—even with the best of intentions.

Despite these acknowledged differences and occasional run-ins, most of us want to spend time with our children and grandchildren even as we recognize that the duration will be somewhat controlled by geographical proximity—no matter how flexible our schedules may have become. Parents who are within a short distance from children and grandchildren may be called on in emergencies for babysitting or car-pooling, or they may drop in for short visits, all of which builds history and creates close ties among all three generations. Sheer proximity invites spontaneous togetherness not available for grandparents who have to travel long distances to be with their families. Some retired couples therefore move closer to their children so they may participate in their lives in meaningful ways by being wanted members of a unit. Doing so, they anticipate an enriched relationship with adult children and look forward to being audiences for their grandchildren's games and performances.

Research has shown that for those anticipations to be met, grandparents must be relatively self sufficient, physically, mentally and socially. One respondent to our questionnaire tells the story of her parents who moved to town after their first visit to her and her husband's new home in Washington. Moving from Minnesota after having made a down payment on a condo in Florida—suggesting a different plan—they rented a house close to their daughter and her family.

Grandmother was content to lead a life there like the one she had always loved, taking care of husband and family and meeting her social needs in their presence or proximity. Grandfather, on the other hand, was an energetic, gregarious man who got involved in the local senior center, a modest structure in its early becoming. He liked the company it offered but thought the facility too humble for existing and future inhabitants. He therefore launched an enterprising and highly successful fund raising campaign for a new and larger center. With the building in place, he looked to activities beyond shooting the breeze and raised money for pool tables and kilns. In between those activities he chauffeured grandchildren about and provided audience and cheers for their games. He was a happy man. Likely, had personal choices effected a reversal of roles—an outgoing grandmother and a family focused grandfather—both would have prospered as well.

That this scenario, the move to be close to family, does not always play out along expected lines, however, many have realized. Those who have disregarded the knowledge that our adult children would like availability on our part but not interference in their lives have done so at their peril. Our children do not want to be responsible for their parents' happiness on a daily basis beyond that which naturally accrues from family togetherness. They expect parents to have lives of their own, even as they wait in the wings to be called on to perform. A tall order.

Whether we are in close proximity to our children or far away, the tension many of us experience between our own agenda, the work or projects we engage in, and our new proclaimed availability for our children and husbands can be resolved only by a determined faith in the worth of our chosen endeavors. Without that, domestic identity and responsibility as well as the need to be loved are likely to tip the scales against personal exploration.

The potential conflict between the two has found rich articulation among professional grandmothers of our generation. Studies at Ohio State University, for example, addressing the ambivalent relationships among adult children and parents rank "ambivalence between autonomy and dependence" first on their list of problematic areas, and most of us have stories to tell of being caught with plane tickets for Europe and receiving a call for help from an adult child whose world is temporarily falling apart due to a break up with a boyfriend, a job opportunity lost, or a car accident leaving physical and monetary bruises. The choice to go or stay is difficult because neither alternative is desirable: give up the trip, forfeit tickets and reservations and, worse than that, incur a potential feeling of guilt and failure on the part of the child who caused the losses; or go on the trip and leave the child in the lurch with the worry and anxiety that go with that decision. A no-win situation, which nonetheless must be resolved one way or the other.

It wasn't always thus. Inga's grandmother's commitment to her grandchildren was total. She had seemingly no agenda of her own. Having lost her husband in the First World War, she spent her life caring for her two children then five and three, and subsequently for her grandchildren. At her daughter's marriage, she moved in with the newlyweds and lived there till she built her own house in the same town. In either location, her primary world was shaped and inhabited by her three grandchildren, who adored her, a grown-up whose entire agenda was ours and who had so much to bring to it. She was a strong, intelligent woman who had held on to her farm at the death of her mate and subsequently sold it in Danish currency rather than the devalued German mark. She consequently had the means to live independently within the circumference of the places she knew. Only on one occasion, when she was seventy-eight years old, did she don her travel clothes and fly over the Pole to Seattle to take care of her baby great-granddaughter whose mother was taking PhD exams. On her arrival at dawn in the Seattle airport she must have read surprise in her granddaughter's face, for she immediately explained her somewhat changed looks by the fact she had cut off her long white hair, ever in a bun, and had had a perm to effect a more manageable hair style so far away from home.

That was a real grandmother. She had chosen to make her life one with ours, at what costs we will never know. But she stayed the course, kept her faith and reaped her reward, the boon all of us may wish for: in our minds and hearts she was irreplaceable.

Today's retired professional women may not be able to effect such congruence of self and others and may continue to experience ambivalence toward the roles of mothering and grandmothering which many of us want to perform without altogether losing time and opportunity for carrying out our self assigned work. Women of our generation were brought up to put family first, and we may feel selfish attending to our own agenda. Yet, except in emergency situations which demand assistance on a full time basis, adult children in general feel relieved at the thought that their aging parents, singly or together, have lives of their own, especially if they are happy in them.

Our children along with the rest of us find satisfaction, vindication even, in knowing or living with people who are fueled by passion and absorbed in their work. Dorothy Canfield Fisher tells the story of Aunt Mehetabel, who "has never for a moment known the pleasure of being important to anyone." Unmarried, she has lived all her adult life with her brother's family and willingly taken on the tedious chores of washing and ironing, cleaning and canning. The family are not unkind, but nor are they caring. To them, Aunt Mehetable is almost invisible in her insignificance to their lives. At the age of sixty-eight, however, Mahetable begins making a quilt so extraordinary she plans to enter it at the County Fair. Suddenly everyone in the family takes notice of her. Her sister-in-law relieves Mehetable of some of her chores, and family participation reaches a crescendo when she is given "for herself a little round table in the sitting room, for her, where she could keep her pieces and use odd minutes for her work."

The quilter is transformed in the process as she feels the "atmosphere of her world" changing. "Now things had a meaning." Five years it takes to complete the quilt, but the first prize is hers, and she feels "like an artist who has realized his ideal." She has effected a balance between nurturing others and nurturing herself, and she has received the respect of both in the process. That is the balance all of us must effect as a recipe for vital relationships: accommodation of our families' agenda with our own, granting of their independence as we grant ours.

Yet another consideration enters the freedom—the mandate even—we have to build a life for ourselves in our retirement phase. " It occurs to me," wrote Carol Ganim, one of the contributors to *Women Confronting Retirement*, "that we as a generation have an obligation to our daughters and their daughters to create models that they might use and adapt in their time. Here is no preexisting model for us; our mothers did not choose their retirement life; they had few changes in their daily lives as they aged. We, on the other hand, must create an economy of retirement, an ecology which will sustain us and our progeny as we grow old in an environment of challenge, peace, activity, productivity, freedom, and generosity ... I feel like Anita Brookner's uncharacteristically active heroine, Fay, in *Brief Lives*, who told herself: 'I should be training for old age, which takes a certain amount of training; better to start as I meant to go on.'"

Fay is right, and one way to "train ourselves" is to practice the balance of autonomy and dependence between generations on neutral grounds where no one and everyone are responsible for the day-to-day details of meals and activities and the resulting free time such mutual responsibility accords. Inga remembers such occasions from Thanksgiving holidays with her family in a rented cabin on the Oregon coast or in the officers' quarters on the parade grounds of Fort Worden in Washington, and Ellie's family has sought them during two weeks at Priest Lake, Idaho every summer since 1965. By now married daughters rent their separate cabins, and family members walk in and out of one another's houses and spend as much time together as they please.

There is no generation gap at Priest Lake, observed Kathleen, when she was ten and had just acquired the term; now her children chime in on the same note. Other families who have rented cabins on the west side of the lake have become extended relations as well as mutual audiences and participants in games and performances enriched and sustained by their own imaginations for lack of televisions and phones. Growing friendships have extended their summer exposures to wedding and birthday celebrations at other times of the year and in different locations lending those all the human warmth and sense of safety we experience when we have multiple hearts, young and old, to draw from. Such exposure combats misrepresentation of any ages, builds compassion and understanding and perhaps teaches us to celebrate one another.

Celebration is the point of Frida Kerner Furman's story in *Facing the Mirror* of a woman who wanted to give her mother a special gift. Frida's mother had retired as a secretary nine years before and in the intervening time had been reading Western classics. Her daughter now wanted to celebrate her accomplishments and show her off as a role model for younger women. So she called some of her own women friends together and all sat down to a traditional "tea." Everyone was asked to introduce herself and briefly reflect on the occasion which had brought them together. Some saw the event as an "inspiration," a model they would try to imitate, and all were moved by the "ritualized acknowledgement of intergenerational relationship" in which they partook with finger sandwiches, trifles, and scones.

Over and over we realize that food does so much more than meet biological needs. A staple of most of the activities mentioned above, it is a social event in which we feed one another and ourselves. Long days of July and August lingering into evenings make special claims for gatherings of family and friends for summer fare. Depending on our numbers and the time we want to spend cooking, we can tailor our offerings to our needs. We can set an easy pace starting out a dinner with gazpacho, for example, moving on to marinated steak and potato salad and finishing any way we like. Eating time no one reckons by the clock, only by the pleasures such time generates.

Our Gazpacho comes with memories of a picnic lunch on the top of Vail Mountain in Colorado. There, it was the first course in a series of delectables and provided a promising beginning for a lazy afternoon. We have served it often, always to raves and satisfaction among partakers.

Gazpacho

½ cucumber
½ mild onion such as Walla Walla or 4 green onions
½ avocado
½ tsp. leaf oregano
3 T olive or salad oil
2 T red wine vinegar
4 cups canned tomato or V8 juice and 1 fresh tomato
2 T fresh lime juice

Add all to blender or Cuisinart and whirl. Add Tabasco and salt to taste.

For a second course in summer we almost always serve marinated steak on the grill and our favorite potato salad.

Marinated Steak for Any Budget

A full cut of round steak, sirloin, London Broil, or Chateaubriand about 1 ½ to 2 inches thick.
Meat tenderizer (as needed—depends on choice of meat)
4 oz of soy sauce
4 oz of Worcestershire sauce
1 package of dried onion soup
Poke holes throughout meat with large fork
Sprinkle generously or sparsely with tenderizer
Pour on 2 oz of soy and Worcestershire sauce each
Add ½ package of onion soup
Repeat on other side of cut.

Refrigerate overnight and turn as often as is convenient. Grill on both sides till done, depending on cut and thickness of meat.

Our Favorite Potato Salad

The amounts of potatoes and onions vary with the size of the group of diners; only the proportion of lemon juice and olive oil remains in proportion of 1 to 2.

New potatoes (e.g. ten average potatoes)
Walla Walla onions or other sweet varieties (e.g. two onions)
1/3 cup of lemon juice
2/3 cup of olive oil
1 bunch parsley

Boil, peel and slice potatoes. Slice onions as thinly as possible and put them in a large, flat dish. Sprinkle heavily with salt and let them drain for about one hour. Wash your hands and squeeze the softened, dripping onions onto several layers of paper towels. Layer potatoes and onions in a flat salad bowl. Pour over both a mixture of lemon juice and olive oil. Mix and cover generously with snipped parsley.

Marinated Steak and *Favorite Potato Salad* have been summer food stand-bys in our families for forty years. They are absolutely foolproof in the making and safe in potential transporting to wherever the dinner is being enjoyed.

Our choice of wine for summer food easily accommodates both tastes and pocket-books. A Washington or California Merlot or a Malbec from Chile or Argentina both fit the occasion. They are young, smooth and fruit forward. For people who prefer French wines of the less fruity variety, a Cote de Rhone, for example a Chateau Neuf de Pape, would be a suitable choice. We have tried all three and found the middle price range—from ten to fifteen dollars—very good indeed.

If the grandchildren's annual outing with grandparents for huckleberry picking at Priest Lake has yielded enough berries to bring home for a pie, we will serve that for a third course.

Huckleberry Pie

Pie Crust for Fresh Fruit Pie :
1 ½ cups flour
1 ½ tsp. sugar
1 tsp. salt
½ cup vegetable oil
2 T. milk

Mix all in a bowl and pat into pie pan. Bake at 425 about 10 minutes.

Huckleberry Glaze:
¾ cup water
1 cup huckleberries
3 T. cornstarch combined with
1 cup sugar
1 tsp. to 1 T lemon juice
3 cups berries

Simmer 1 cup berries in water for 3 to 4 minutes. Add sugar and starch to cooking fruit. Stirring frequently, cook till syrup is thick and ruby clear. Add lemon juice. Cool slightly. Add 3 cups berries to cooled piecrust. Pour sauce over berries.

If huckleberries are scarce, however, or the eating has been too enthusiastic for a baking yield, we have a fallback position which some think equally delectable and perhaps more unusual as it features a combination of memory and inspiration prompted by local produce. All through her childhood, on August fourteenth, Inga would attend a birthday party at the house of a classmate in the little town where she grew up. From year to year, she'd look forward to the special apple tart her friend's mother made like no one else and which for her contained the essence of mid August's apple flavors and pungent hints of fall. In their more southerly location, Yakima apricots similarly hold all of summer in their tawny skins and therefore invite a like baking venture. So, Inga invented a combination more tart than the remembered apple temptation and therefore gentled with a layer of custard between the piecrust and the apricot filling.

Apricot Tart

Pie Crust for All Occasions:
¼ pound butter or margarine
1½ cups flour
¼ cup sugar
1 egg beaten with cold water to make about ½ cup

Add butter and one cup of flour to Cuisinart, or crumble with fingers. With Cuisinart running, add the egg and water mixture and enough flour to form a ball. Refrigerate. Roll out the dough on a floured surface and cut a round to fit the pie plate. Cut the remaining dough in strips and use one to rim the edge of the pie plate. Reserve the rest for the lattice to be put on top of the apricot filling.

Simple Vanilla Custard

4 T flour
1 T cornstarch
1/3 cup sugar
Pinch of salt
2 cups milk
2 eggs
1 T vanilla
1 dab of butter

Add first five ingredients to saucepan. Turn heat to medium and stir till bubbles form. Beat the two eggs and add to mixture. Keep stirring and cooking till more bubbles form. Remove from heat and add vanilla and butter. If this recipe yields more custard than the tart requires, stir the remainder into a bowl of whipped cream and serve on top of berries or ice cream.

Apricot Filling

1 pound apricots
Enough water to start the cooking
3 to 4 T of sugar or more to taste.

Cook apricots with water to make a tart compote. Add sugar to taste.
Spread custard in piecrust. Spread cooked apricots on top. Make lattice of reserved pie dough and bake at 350 till crust is golden. About 45 minutes.

We can all follow recipes if we put our minds to the task, and cooking is less an art than an attitude. It's to our benefit, we think, to develop a sensible attitude toward cooking and eating. We can decide we like to eat our own cooking and like to treat friends to it as an occasion for comfort, fun, and conversation, or we may enjoy certain aspects of food preparation such as reading cookery books, setting tables, or presenting colorful arrangements of fruits and vegetables. On the other hand, we may decide to cook as little as possible and combat the sneaking sense of guilt such a decision may evoke; especially if our mates enjoy dining on home cooked victuals. In such a case, the chore may be shared. Richard Atcheson's ARRP article "Taking the Plunge" shows the way. Give cooking a try, he says. Try something new. In retirement we are our own agents, creating our own options from which we are free to choose. We may cook, nurture, return to part-time employment or sign up for volunteer activity. The important thing is to perceive the possibilities, choose the ones that will work for us and take responsibility for our subsequent actions.

So far, the ways of spending our time presented and discussed here all lie within the "worlds" we know and in which we have an established identity: salaried or volunteered part-time work or family related activities. Other realms beckon with options we may or may not have imagined. One is the world of books, which is increasingly open to all of us in text and tapes even as eyes are dimming and ears are clogging up. If we have not learned before and our inclinations run in that direction, we may now set out to become real readers. The literature we choose is determined by the purpose—or purposes—we lend it. Most professional women have read for professional purposes, to pass exams, bone up for interviews, or deliver lectures. Those are ready made, clearly articulated goals with objectives designed and formulated by institutions or individuals.

To be good readers when we have no professional obligations to fulfill, we need an internal purpose of sorts. All of us know about "pleasure reading" for distraction or escape from career or family obligations. We can read like Maureen in Nadine Gordimer's *July's People* about a white South African family taking refuge with their black servant in his native village. In their haste to leave, the wife and mother of the family has brought only one novel to read, and she finds the story "unable to offer competition" to the life she is attempting to fashion among July's people. A shallow liberal thinker and lukewarm revolutionary, Maureen is shown to be a superficial reader as well, whose reading habits reflect her lifelong inability, or unwillingness, to read and interpret the text of her life as a privileged white woman in a predominantly black society. She ultimately runs away from July's village as her thoughts have always fled the issues of her world. Had she been able to read, Gordimer implies by Maureen's choice of *The Betrothed* by Allessandro Manzoni, she might have learned about cowardice and consequence in the seemingly sporadic and insignificant actions of man, and she might have stood her ground instead of fleeing toward a landing helicopter propelled by enemy or friendly forces. The imagery at the end of the novel suggests Zeus's rape of Leda whom he visits in the guise of a swan, a mating which gives birth to Helen of Troy and the disasters in the wake of abrogated responsibility to self and home.

Maureen's failure to learn from her reading about herself and her place in the world should not suggest that reading for distraction or pure pleasure has no value. On the contrary, we are fortune's favorites if we never lose our capacity for absorption in a good story. Page turning prompted by an irresistible text is a joyful activity. Deep down satisfaction from reading, however, as a reward of work, is not derived by remaining on a plateau of ease or planned distraction.

Should we need a mentor for our reading activities, we might consider Yale professor Harold Bloom—one of the most widely read literary critics of our day and with a canonical bias to match the achievement. Bloom is elegiac in his lament that children who grow up with television and go on to computers will never become readers, and he offers a set of national guidelines for a return to reading as education and pastime: *Clear your mind of cant. Do not attempt to improve your neighbor or your neighborhood by what or how you read. A scholar is a candle which the love and desire of all men will light. One must be an inventor to read well. Recover the ironic.* Sensible dictums all.

Musing on these principles, Bloom furthermore teaches us—perhaps inadvertently—the degree of alertness a real reader must bring to the text. He bases his pronouncements on the contention that genuine literacy means having some familiarity with a number of standard texts and an ability to spot irony. Yet irony cannot be taught, he insists. "With this principle I am close to despair, since you can no more teach someone to be ironic than you can instruct them to become solitary. And yet the loss of irony is death of reading, and of what had been civilized in our natures." If we read *How to Read and Why* carefully, however, we may discover that Bloom may temper his despair because he himself teaches irony by example.

A look at the second principle, "do not attempt to improve your neighbor or your neighborhood by what or how you read," reveals a delicious irony between text and subtext. The text argues that we read so we may know ourselves and our worlds, and the subtext suggests that reading the author's interpretations of his readings, we improve our reading habits and rescue our brains from the maw of the television-to-computer travesty of civilization. It is unlikely Bloom would laud that take on his text, instead preferring to see his function as that of a candle lit by the "love and desire of all men." He is that candle, but like most teachers, he occasionally hoists himself by his own petard.

All the same, if we set ourselves up for mentorship with an appropriately skeptical attitude, we may learn from Bloom to read, as he puts it, "to strengthen the self and learn its authentic interests." Few of us read *Moby Dick* at nine years old as he recalls doing, thus making an early start at becoming a serious reader. Yet some of us will remember spending our childhood summers enlarging our worlds through books providing private space and sacred communication between reader and writer. Likely we, too, graduated from "youth" literature to classics, a progression which comes naturally to an alert reader as her mind becomes sated with fluff and demands increasingly chewier grist.

Inga remembers the summer her daughter, then in middle school, on returning from days spent with a friend at the Washington seashore, burst into the house declaring, "Mother I'm done with Harlequin romances." Years later, finishing her junior year in high school and having fulfilled most graduation requirements, the same child announced herself ready to accept a Rotary scholarship for a year abroad and yet graduate with her class on the grounds that she had met the requirements and, besides, had read "all the books in the school library." Her words found resonance in the consciousness of her mother who remembered with undiminished clarity how as a junior in high school she had pronounced herself "croupy" so she might stay in bed till the end of *Anna Karenina*. Seventeen-year-old Inga had reasoned that school on any given day held no more important lesson than Tolstoy's novel of love, betrayal, and consequences.

Books can go a long way toward making us aware of what we feel even as we recreate what a masterful writer has felt. Because we are ourselves and not the author, however, we must go one step further: leave our guide behind and continue on our own. Marcel Proust was an ardent admirer and translator of Ruskin, the English art historian, but eventually he left translating behind and ventured into his own realm with *Remembrance of Things Past*. His work on Ruskin had taught him to make a distinction between "conclusions" which the author arrived at and presented in his work and "incitements" which the reader experiences as a consequence. The reader's wisdom, he would assert, "begins where the author leaves off." Writers do not provide answers; they only "generate desires." They can introduce us to the spiritual life, but their texts do not *constitute* that life. Toward that, we must ourselves take the necessary steps, learn to really read.

An avid reader from childhood and disinclined toward outdoor activities, Proust had realized the temptation to read as a substitute for active engagement in the process of living. He warns against that. "As long as reading is for us the instigator whose magic keys have opened the door to those dwelling-places deep within us that we would not have known how to enter, its role in our lives is salutary. It becomes dangerous, on the other hand, when, instead of awakening us to the personal life of the mind, reading tends to take its place, when the truth no longer appears to us as an ideal which we can realize only by the intimate progress of our own thought and the efforts of our heart, but as something material, deposited between the leaves of books like a honey fully prepared by others and which we need only take the trouble to reach down from the shelves of libraries and then sample passively in a perfect repose of mind and body."

Implicit in his warning is a caveat against the kind of "self help" book that promises cures for our ills if we will only ingest their "honey" as "fully prepared." Prescriptive texts, Proust argues, are not of a kind to offer options for contemplation, make us examine problems in all their aspects and directions, and urge us to let ideas penetrate into our unconscious so the mind may work on them even when they are not objects of our specific focus.

As a way of spending time in retirement, reading, by those lights, would appear a good investment. Writing is a related activity. The two are at home in the same "world." If our aim for reading is discovery of our own natures and deepest desires, writing about our lives will yield similar knowledge and insights. It helps—even as it hurts—to take stock of ourselves and bring to our pasts the broader perspective we must trust our advancing years have afforded. Many of us have probably experienced the release we discover if we can make ourselves write journals in times of special stresses. Getting our suffering, doubts and troubles down on paper, articulating them so we may see them outside ourselves, somehow makes them more manageable, more arrangeable in some kind of pattern or sequence which may lead to catharsis.

"We travel through life guided by an inner plot," writes Jill Kerr Conway, "part the creation of family, part the internalization of a broader social norm, part the function of our imaginations and our own capacity for insight into ourselves, part from our groping to understand the universe in which the planet we inhabit is a speck ... we are all unique, and so are our stories. We should pay close attention to our stories ... search for the ways we experience life differently from the inherited version and edit the plot accordingly, keeping our eyes on the philosophical implications of the changes we make. Was this action free? Was that one determined?"

Writing memoirs or autobiographies will help us see the plot we have lived and divine the forces that shaped it. Clearly or dimly we may begin to see cause and effect and evaluate our agency—or lack of it—in shaping our fate. That, we know, is the first step toward effecting the changes we may want to make in our lives. It buys us eligibility in the race between maturity and senility. A mature person will imagine her future in accordance with acquired perception of her past and steer a different course if needed. She may realize that she has consistently seen herself as a victim, sacrificed by people, environment, or moral codes and wearing the mantle of resignation through a world where some are more equal than others. Or she may, on careful reflection, decide that she has done her best according to available knowledge at the time and her best judgment of the situation. She has created options, made choices in her life, and likely will continue to do so within the vagaries of growing older.

The former scenario may demand profound change of orientation and habits; the latter requires continued adaptation to new situations, illustrated again by the littlepeople and the mice in Spencer Johnson's *Who Moved My Cheese*. The "victimized" littlepeople refused for the longest time to become agents of their own destinies and almost died of that attitude, unlike the mice who re-discovered their ability to forage for opportunity as conditions changed.

Yet another realm of exploration for meaningful work and time well spent is that of the out-of-doors. Walking, hiking, playing tennis or golf, swimming or bird watching may all be considered "work" if we bring to them as much zest as our bodies permit, all the focus and attention our brains can generate, and an irrepressible hope of improvement—or maintenance at least—no matter how old we are. With that combination of forces and investment of time, an interesting and somewhat unexpected reward may come our way. Because we no longer have to "win" or to "qualify" for participation or prove anything to anyone, we can discover the spiritual dimension of a physical activity like walking, which Thoreau decided required "a direct dispensation from heaven," a boon we are granted as we no longer report to work.

We can play tennis or golf, and for that matter, bridge or mahjongg, and enjoy our participation in the game, grateful to have the powers to be out on the courts or at the tables at all. It may take work to arrive at that stance in a culture that drives its children to win and where ten year olds are "drafted" to local baseball teams. But our aging bodies will lead the way toward that recognition and we may arrive and find we are fortunate indeed.

May Sarton understood the spiritual dimension of participation in physical activity and mental agility as she demonstrates with her depiction of two elderly dancers who watch a ballet from their balcony. Initially they are dismayed at the difference between their aging abilities and the strength and litheness of the leaping bodies. Yet before the dance is over, they realize that,

> … in the flesh those dancers cannot spare
> What the old lovers have had time to learn,
> That the soul is a lithe and serene athlete
> That deepens touch upon the darkening air.
> It is not energy but light they burn,
> The radiant powers of the Paraclete.

Sarton had learned what the writers of the Gnostic Gospels knew—that the Paraclete, Holy Spirit, is the life and activity of the divine in nature as well as in and through people. That light need never be extinguished. It has fuel to last for all our days.

As a gardener as well as a writer, Sarton herself demonstrated that kind of ardor. Gardening brought her outside her house and temporarily outside herself, as it does the rest of us. It demands attention and commitment to growth and for the time we invest offers rewards which have appealed to mankind since the biblical Eden and Nebuchadnezzar's Hanging Gardens of Babylon in sixth century BC. By some instinct, we know that flower gardens, vegetable gardens, potted gardens on city roofs or balconies offer both mental and physical stimulation.

Science and literature bear us out. A garden article in a recent *Economist* magazine featured a "life satisfaction by regularity of gardening" chart showing that people who garden "at least once a week" were twice as likely to consider themselves "completely satisfied" as those who tend the soil only "once a month" and three times likelier than those who "never or almost never" put dibble in earth. Calling it "a lovesome thing," the writer touts gardening as being on the increase everywhere in the twenty-first century, from country gardens to city allotments and pots on balconies or city roofs. "Despite relentless urbanization, slums and high-rise housing, more homes have gardens, and gardening is easier than ever before. Moreover, in the countries of the rich world, a generation of baby-boomers is now reaching late middle age and the early years of retirement: just the point at which people's enthusiasm for gardening appears to reach a crescendo. As humanity ages, the planet is likely to be increasingly populated by fervent gardeners."

Literature has long sung the praise of gardens. Voltaire's ironic masterpiece *Candide,* for example, shows a hero who after experiencing the world of travel and adventures visits the garden of a simple Turkish family on the outskirts of Constantinople. After feeding on homemade sherbets and delectable fruits grown on the premises, Candide comments that his host must possess huge and splendid properties. "I have only twenty acres," replies the Turk; I cultivate them with my children, and the work keeps us from three great evils, boredom, vice and poverty." As Candide ponders this reply, he concludes that the Turk was living a life preferable to that of six kings with whom he had recently dined, and the story ends with his acquired conviction that, right or wrong, "we must cultivate our garden." He had been shown that the source of genuine vitality lies not in power to control but in healthy skepticism, individual creativity and free choice.

Voltaire's maxim was taken quite literally by many of the women we interviewed on the topic of gardening. Among them is Joan, who grows her own tomatoes from seed and puts in several hours in her garden every day from spring seeding through summer watering and feeding, into fall's cutting away and composting. The spiritual satisfaction she gains from those life hours among growing plants may not find expression in Mark Twain's belief that a garden is the best place to find God because we can dig for Him there, but neither Joan nor anyone else would contest that work which prevents boredom, vice and poverty is anything but significant.

Meaningful work, then, may be accomplished in the indoor world of reading and writing as well as in the outdoor realm of gardening or other physical activities. To those worlds, we would add that of art in the widest sense of the word. They are fortunate who have made lifelong excursions into that realm and in retirement can extend the duration and frequency of the outings. But the rest of us may start the journey as well. We have lived to see almost any handicraft be labeled "art" and perhaps viewed some outcomes with disparagement, but such skepticism need not bar us entrance. Art forms may be any we want to assign the label and may have in them room for all of us to experiment. Painting, sculpting, drawing, writing, sewing, quilting, playing an instrument, or making a scrapbook are examples.

If throughout our careers we have postponed engagement in artistic pursuits, always meaning to take up one or the other "later," we would be wise to realize that "later" has arrived. The time is now or potentially never, no matter how dubious we are about our ability, how uncertain of success. We know that giving full attention to a task yields inestimable practice and proves gainful even if we temporarily lose heart. One failed effort will train us for pursuit of another, and we have learned long ago that persistence is the mother of success.

Some of us may have to search for a while to find the work to which we can bring both passion and commitment and which will result in a reason for being, a measure of satisfaction, even happiness. Yet we know that the focus and seriousness with which we approach and pursue our perceived and chosen options and the willing attitude we bring to the task are commensurate with the rewards we will reap. For rewards there will be although they may not turn out to be exactly the kinds we imagined.

3

From "Givens" to "Unknowns" in Social Relationships

"[Women] must make the voyage of life alone, and for safety in an emergency, they must know something of the laws of navigation. To guide our own craft, we must be captain, pilot, engineer; with chart and compass to stand at the wheel; to watch the winds and waves, and know when to take in the sail, and to read the signs in the firmament over all ...

In age, when the pleasures of youth are passed ... The more fully faculties of the mind are developed and kept in use, the longer the period of vigor and active interest in all around us continues

— Elizabeth Cady Stanton's farewell speech on resigning as president of the National American Woman Suffrage Association, 1892.

To assume responsibility for ourselves and our work and balance that with social intercourse is a challenge. In our career lives, social contact with colleagues, clients, customers, students or patients was an integral part of functioning in the market place. For some, in fact, interaction with colleagues and co-workers became a primary source and outlet for socialization which we miss when it is no longer a part of our days. For others, such relationships were less gratifying. For all, however, professional social intercourse was a given that not only invited but required our participation.

In our retirement lives, other people's company ceases to be a necessity dictated by professional conventions. It becomes a privilege we may shun or invite. We are free to choose solitude or society or a mixture of the two.

Solitude is not easily achieved—either for lack of time spent alone or for too much of it, which may bring loneliness instead—nor is it highly valued in today's world of much prized global communication. May Sarton flinched at Carolyn Heilbrun's remark that her best writing concerned the topic of solitude. Sarton wanted the laurels for insights into self and human relations. Even so, her journals repeatedly point to solitude as an absolute. "There is no doubt that solitude is a challenge and to maintain balance within it a precarious business. But I must not forget that, for me, being with people or even with one beloved person for any length of time without solitude is even worse. I lose my center. I feel dispersed, scattered in pieces. I must have time alone in which to mull over any encounter, and to extract its juice, its essence, to understand what has really happened to me as a consequence of it."

Sarton knew that to live contented lives, we must look beyond the facts of experience to the meaning behind it, a feat demanding analysis, candor and the courage it takes to transform into solitude the loneliness we all experience as eternal strangers on the earth, homesick and afraid of the dark. For solitude to be born, we must suffer loneliness. That is the cost of "extracting the juice" from our living in the world. Mary Morrison addresses that process in her book *Let Evening Come*. "Being alone," she writes with a borrowing from *King Lear*, "makes me realize what a poor naked wretch I am, what a basic emptiness I am, how it takes all the resources of the outward world to keep me going—books, radio, the fire in the fireplace, food, letters in the mailbox. And I wish I had the courage and the endurance simply to stay completely empty and see what comes to me out of the emptiness. And it feels as if most of the sins and crimes of the human race have risen out of desperately trying to cover that nakedness and avoid that emptiness. Well, but then there is some ecstasy too, when something does fill the emptiness, when all your surroundings speak to you in love, the sun really shines, the rain really falls ... "

Writing in her eighties, Morrison has come to see the rewards as well as the costs of learning to keep oneself company. Celebrating the sun and rain speaking to her in love, she shows herself a pupil of Thoreau, the great American solitary who in his entire life needed only three chairs, two for himself and a friend and three for society. He has fallen out of fashion in a time which urges wider exposure, but Morrison knows her *Walden* and echoes the author's conviction that "the most sweet and tender, the most innocent and encouraging society may be found in any natural object, even for the poor misanthrope and most melancholy man. There can be no very black melancholy to him who lives in the midst of Nature and has his senses still."

Living in the midst of nature has an archaic ring to it. It suggests a distancing from the culture of the land with its commercialism, bureaucracy and conformity, and it prompts a question about the kind of social modes we might imagine, which would encourage the loneliness of individuation as a desirable developmental goal. Moving toward such a goal would involve toleration of a certain estrangement from the mainstream of activity as we strive for meaning in our lives, as well as an understanding of solitude as either a deceptively easy way out or a well-considered option. Choosing it would mean a deliberate effort to live a life into which friends are invited and welcome, but which ultimately depends on oneself for fulfillment of needs.

We know of a woman, Emily, a dean in a Washington community college, who retired with her husband, a fellow dean, to a farmhouse some miles out of town. While still in their sixties, they rode horses. He grew a large garden with corn and potatoes and roses as she discontinued membership in the women's organizations to which she had belonged, kept up her cooking and cleaning and read newspapers, *The New Yorker* and *Atlantic Monthly* as well as books on biological sciences, which was her field of interest and expertise. As she had always done, Emily invited select friends for dinner and would occasionally treat former colleagues to a lunch featuring the world's best biscuits kept warm in a linen lined basket, green beans from the garden, expertly fried chicken and delectable apple pies. She and her husband were also glad to be invited back and would come dressed in the well tailored suits they had worn in their teaching and administrative days.

Emily outlived her husband by almost twenty years, staying in the farm house reading her magazines and keeping up with the news, enjoying the visits of friends and colleagues, her two sons and their children, and appearing on the whole content in her self generated solitude. She stayed the course through diabetes and increasing frailness, turning a deaf ear to any suggestions or conversations proposing she move into town and a condominium which would demand less upkeep than her farm house, offer companionship beyond her cat and infrequent drop-ins of friends, and provide more readily available aid should the need arise. She did not resent the upkeep, didn't desire additional company and thought herself independent of aid.

Throughout the time we knew her, she exhibited two modes of behavior, represented by her tailored suits for work and social events outside her home and the levis and work shirts she wore in her life at the farm house, formal and informal as the occasion demanded. Those were her face to the world, and they served her well.

When illness forced her into hospital and subsequent nursing home care, she donned an unfamiliar, "institutional" garb, lost her moorings and died within a year. Emily had lived a life dedicated to personal values. She had spent little on herself and much on seeing her grandchildren through school because she wanted to give them the best odds for living a contented life: continuous learning. She had cared little for crowds and trends and opinions of the day, but she remained unfailingly loyal to her friends and to the life she had chosen, unafraid to stick to her story and remaining most "respectable" in her solitude, exactly as Elisabeth Cady Stanton imagined it. "If a woman feels responsible," she wrote, "her solitude will be ...respectable and she will not be driven to gossip or scandal for entertainment."

To our knowledge, Emily did not experience alienation from mainstream and society because, unlike most of us, she appeared to crave neither audience nor recognition. That many of us do, we attribute to the fact that in our professional lives we had both. We have come to take for granted being sought out, listened to, and respected for our knowledge and the status it confers. Only gradually do we discover that the world's acknowledgement is no longer ours. Some professional women retain their audiences in retirement as they work part time, but most arrive at the realization that the world is not likely to come knocking at our doors. That knowledge does not stifle our need, but it does present us with the options of relegating the longing for listeners to the realm of daydreams or making our retired and transformed talents and beings worth seeking out.

Primary examples of lives in the realm of fantasizing are many of Anita Brookner's quiet existences, men and women alike. Her novels are set in contemporary England, and in her latest work, *Making Things Better*, she tells of Julius Herz who, in his retirement, wishes he had an audience who would value his life experiences. He imagines appearing on television and being addressed by a sympathetic interviewer, a fantasy many of us may give a nod of recognition.

"What he could imagine would be himself discoursing on the persistence of early memory, of images that had stayed with him throughout his life. He would be seen, on the success of such a performance, to be worth consulting in the interests of general enlightenment, would go on—always with encouragement—to describe the Casino at Baden-Baden, its rich debased rococo decoration so perfectly suited to the spirit of the place, or more ambitious than this, to give an account of his travels, of his artistic delight, Schloss Bruhl, near Cologne, or the house that Wittgenstein designed for his sister in Vienna. Asked back yet again he would be memorable on the Claudes and Turners in the National Gallery, on which his opinion would prove invaluable. These were matters on which he had reflected in the course of his evening walks, but on which he was obliged to remain mute. The existence of such an audience remained his most persistent temptation. His real audience became as strange to him as the people in the supermarket ... Such indifference, with which he was obliged to conform, remained the order of the day."

The wistful tone of the paragraph suggests the ephemeral nature of Herz's - Heart's - unfulfilled longing for meaningful participation in the world and its affairs as it signals his lacking incentive and stamina. As such, his "case" forms an interesting, and perhaps disquieting, counterpart to the many case histories with which magazines and self-help texts will convince us that we, too, can—ought to—succeed in repackaging ourselves and be worthy of company.

If we find neither the isolation of solitude or fantasyland, nor the frantic involvement of undirected "business" appealing, we might seek a middle course, constituting a balance of the two. Doing that depends on our willingness to go beyond daydreaming to transforming the talent and knowledge we used in our careers along the line of individual inclination and energy.

That social relationships matter was evidenced in the responses we received to our questionnaire. Asked the extent to which retired professional women found social contacts in the workplace satisfactory, the majority, sixty–three percent, answered "great"; only thirty-seven percent said "moderate"; no one checked the "not at all" box.

The majority furthermore admitted to missing the social contacts that were part and parcel of their employment world. The degree of their loss, great, moderate or not at all, seemed to depend primarily on whether or not retirement had been succeeded by moving to another town. As one woman put it, "I am a people person. I can meet people easily. What I miss are those relationships with a history. As a retired woman in a new community, I am viewed differently from the way I would have been perceived had I still been working. Moving also makes networking difficult. It would have been easier if I had remained in the Portland area." A fellow respondent who has stayed in her hometown supports her contention, "I see long-time friends everywhere I go in Yakima. I was born here," and, we may add, recognized here for the work she did.

In addition to geographical location, employment history also influences the nature and degree of women's loss of social interaction and relationships provided in the work place. An Ohio State University study found that fifty percent of the retired women surveyed missed the daily social contacts their work environment had provided. As one woman put it, "When you're working you have ... people you see everyday and you really miss them ... I felt lonely, a lot because I had worked around so many people." Another missed easily obtained information about local and national current events, "I missed being there and talking ... and also knowing what was going on 'cause there we kept up with what was happening." Professional women in this study specifically stressed their loss of social interactions in "the context of their former professions,"that is, related to their career attachment and history and therefore not resolved merely by continued social contacts with former colleagues who move on without them.

In retirement, we, too, must move on because most of us are not misanthropes. We know that our environments and the people in them play a role in our journeys toward self knowledge as echoes of our natures and expectations and as playing fields for the good we may be able to effect in the world as self appointed workers, volunteers or family members. We mentioned earlier that loss of environmental echoes is Isak Dinesen's plangent lament during her first years back in Denmark following her displacement from Africa. To a historical revisionist, her view of the native squatters and servants bears the imprint of colonial superiority, and no doubt the childless baroness found satisfaction in tending and educating the native young. That does not, however, invalidate her view that at least where women are concerned, the presence of echoes in their environs is vital to their happiness. In Africa, she saw herself as useful, making a difference in the world where she had placed herself. So unlike the pitiful divorcee, wracked by disease, who had returned to the shelter of her mother's house.

Contemporary social scientists support Dinesen's claim. They report that women in general know, by instinct or other lights, that finding human response is a condition for well-being. Basing their argument on recent research, they refute the generally accepted knowledge that confronted with stress, humans will either fight or fly. Two women scientists at UCLA conducted a study, *Female Responses to Stress: Tend and Befriend, Not Fight or Flight*, contending that "women respond to stress with a cascade of brain chemicals that cause us to make and maintain friendships with other women." They had discovered that women respond to stress differently from men, on whom ninety percent of stress research has been focused.

This difference may play a significant role for our health and longevity, they alleged, as it appears that when stress releases the hormone oxytocin in women, it counteracts the "fight and flight" impulse and instead encourages us to tend children or call our women friends. That behavior, in contrast to the male response of producing large amounts of testosterone, which reduces the mollifying effects of oxytocin, encourages a "tend and befriend" action which strengthens rather than weakens body and soul.

It follows from that—and research supports the contention—that women, by and large, are willing to spend considerable time and energy on forming networks, maintaining friendships, and engaging in emotionally intimate relationships with other women. They have internalized the mantra that sociologists and medical scientists have long been repeating: with friends we not only live longer but better, more joyfully.

Asked how they planned to transform the social relationships that were a "given" in their employment lives into relationships in the "worlds" in which they would live and work in retirement, our questionnaire respondents mentioned explorations in one or more of the five realms outlined in Chapter Two. As we demonstrated by discussion and examples, two of those—salaried or volunteered part time work and family engagement—offer ready-made "worlds" peopled by colleagues, fellow volunteers, or family members. The remaining three: reading and writing, the out-of-doors, and arts and crafts are more problematic. They demand sustained efforts toward establishing a venue for performance and social relationships because although they may offer familiar outlines from earlier forays, those realms are less likely to be initially substantive in either shape, content, or direction.

Making them "worlds" for our engagement, therefore, will demand greater commitment and more willing suspension of safety. It is risky to try our hands in new fields of endeavor because we cannot know the outcome. We may fall flat on our faces, but as James Thurber noted, that is no worse than falling over backwards in avoidance. If on retirement we acknowledge our freedom to set sails for unknown destinations, we cannot escape their corollary of risk. A vignette from Emma Donogue's *The Woman Who Gave Birth to Rabbits* puts the exclamation mark to that observation:

'What sort of God lets these things happen,' [one young Quaker woman asks another as they watch a shipwreck].

'These things, meaning wrecks,' asked Anna harshly.

'Yes,' said Sarah, 'and other things,' her eyes on her cousin's motionless knees, skinny as a dog under their blanket.

Anna kept staring out at the splintering ship. 'The same God who made the seas for us to sail on,' she said finally.

'But'

'We can't have it both ways,' snapped her cousin. 'Either we are free, or we are safe; take your pick.'

Different pursuits hold different amounts of risk. It is less risky to try becoming a good reader than becoming a good writer. Training for a marathon is riskier than working up to daily walks. Painting in watercolors is more challenging than putting together a collage, and yet who is to say which of those pursuits is the more satisfactory in terms of either personal reward or social relationships? How are we to know for sure what we might become enthusiastic about or who will ignite our passion?

Understanding ourselves and our potential may come mysteriously if we give it a chance. Dante's lovely lines in *Purgatorio* liken such insights to the green leaves emerging from a plant:

Every substantial form, which is at once
distinct from matter and united with it,
has a specific virtue stored within it

known only by its operation
and revealed by the effect it has,
as the green leaves reveal the life of a plant.

And so, nobody knows where it comes from,
the understanding of first ideas,
or the fondness for the first object of passion;

they are in you, as the need to make honey
is in the bee, for this primary
urge there is no place either for praise or blame.

In the loss we may experience as we depart our careers is the
seed of its transformation as a need within us warranting neither
applause nor censure.

Some pursuits may appear to have in them more staying power
and social exchange than others, and likely do, but that will become
clear only in the process of engagement, and we are free to make
another choice at any time. If we move to Florida, we can move
back again or somewhere else. Nor do we have to dispute the worth
of those pursuits—or of ourselves—as we implement our choices.
As our own arbiters and evaluators, we need only take responsibility for our choice of work and the standards we set for its performance. Emerson has departed the stage of our national consciousness along with his friend Thoreau, but from time to time a
sentence or two from his essay on self-reliance rings out from the
wings. "There is a time in every man's education," he warns,
"when he arrives at the conviction that envy is ignorance; that
imitation is suicide; that he must take himself for better for worse
as his portion ... The power which resides in him is new in nature,
and none but he knows what that is which he can do, nor does he
know until he has tried."

Nor can we, retired professional women, individually or
collectively, know what we can make of ourselves and our relation-

ships until we exert our powers. We must build the road as we go and remember we are not alone. Our ranks are swelling. In the next ten years, the oldest of the baby boomers will be in their early sixties, and people aged sixty-five and older already comprise the most rapidly increasing segments of the American population. In the course of twenty years, the number of women in the U.S. labor force has increased in proportions never seen before.

In 1999, sixty percent of women worked outside their homes. It follows that as time goes on, women will retire in numbers equal to those of their male counterparts. What does not necessarily follow is that a proportionate number of women will be or will become professional women. But the trend is moving in that direction. In fall quarter 2002 the University of Washington and Washington State University reported a gender breakdown for undergraduates at fifty-two percent women to forty-eight percent men, and over a recent six-year span, seventy-three percent women graduated whereas only sixty-three percent male students finished their degrees. At present, fifty-seven percent of BA's, forty-three percent of doctors, forty-nine percent of lawyers, and sixty-nine percent of veterinarians are women. Of more immediate interest in this context, women now make up sixty percent of the sixty-five-and-over population in the United States. By 2010, almost half of adult women will be at least fifty. More and more imaginations will be put to the task of making the Third Stage the most fulfilling in terms of expansion of consciousness and unalloyed gratitude for every day our eyes can see, brains can function, bodies can move—to whatever degree.

With that dimension of gratitude in our lives, all experience acquires a spiritual dimension and we learn as we go the difference between "wanting to win" and "having to win." Wanting to "win"—succeed in our self engendered work—we will do our best and it will be good enough because we choose our tasks in accordance with our natures and in mute conspiracy with all those other imaginations who make up our "cohort" of professional women. That is more important than beating our opponent on the tennis court or even securing an audience for our artwork, however satisfactory that is. Our work will show us who we are, regardless of outcome. The lost tennis game, the unpublished memoirs, the undisplayed painting, the unheard sonata all have life for us. All tell our stories.

Depending on their nature, some of our pursuits will be solitary endeavors. Others may be translated into social relationships. Reading, for example, on the surface a solitary activity, may be given a social dimension by enlistment of like-minded others. Twenty years ago, several women who wanted to establish a "salon" for readers to rekindle the intellectual stimulation they had experienced in college or careers asked Inga to set up a reading group with the goal of reading books which participants were unlikely to read by themselves. To be "inclusive" and discourage sign-ups by readers who would join because it was "the trend" or the "in-thing" to do, Inga suggested that anyone interested sign up for a class, "Writers and Ideas," at the local college. The "students" would register for credits or as audits, and Inga would "teach" the two-credit course, that is, lead the discussions during the ten meetings of two annual sessions coinciding with fall and winter quarters of the academic year. Participants would take turns hosting the group.

This system worked well, until in one quarter the sign-up exceeded the number most drawing rooms could comfortably contain. So after one quarter in a college classroom—without the coffee and cookies to which the group had become accustomed—the "class" decided to break away from the college but to keep up the "tuition" to ensure Inga's continued leadership of the meetings.

Twenty years later we have read our way through the English canon from Defoe's *Moll Flanders* to Pat Barker's World War I trilogy, studied the tradition of drama from Sophocles to Samuel Beckett, marveled at the richness of Scandinavian masterpieces previously unknown to most Readers, exercised our minds to contain Thomas Mann's *Doctor Faustus*, a feat almost as daunting as Joyce's *Ulysses* and nearly matched by Henry James, whom we included in our American canon. We have read the great Russians and become part of the French tradition from Madame De Lafayette via Balzac, Stendahl, Flaubert and Proust, on to Sartre and Camus.

We choose our texts by consensus: a certain country's literature, an era, a genre or a theme, or we agree to honor requests made for specific works by individual Readers, who lobby persuasively enough to convince the group of their choice.

One woman in her eighties insisted we read Marcel Proust before she grew one season older and lost the acumen she deemed necessary for the task. Time will show how far we make it into Proust's many volumed *Remembrance,* but we have agreed to make a start and take it on faith– as we have done before—that we can learn to read "what comes near to ourself, what we can put to use" as the eighteenth century English lexicographer Samuel Johnson phrased it. It may be a stretch with a text like Proust's, but mental stretching is a by-law of this organization. Our rewards are continuous, as Virginia Woolf so convincingly imagines in her encounter with Saint Peter at the Pearly Gates. He is meting out the just deserts of the latest arrivals, she writes, and he sees us coming with our books and decides we need no further rewards. "They loved to read."

Reading groups make attractive markets for publishers and authors of books offering advice and do's and don'ts about such organizations. Our experience has taught us that having someone, preferably knowledgeable, assume leadership of discussions and be present at all meetings provides continuity and focus. Those may also be achieved, however, if the group can agree on a theme, a period, a genre or other common denominators for the course of study. Concentration on an agreed upon objective beats random readings or "best-seller hopping" because it allows participants to make connections between works, aids in remembering the readings, and trains our facilities for pattern recognition and comparisons. Developing those, we become a reading group rather than a book club.

Depending on the readers as well as the agreed upon purpose, the reading group's social and psychological aspects may be as important as the rendered intellectual stimulation. Because it is easier and less uncomfortable to discuss personal issues couched in literary characters and events, individual members may raise questions and offer comments on a book under discussion without revealing their personal nature.

In the course of years then, participants assume the habits of analysis and in-depth discussions pertaining to individual matters and public concerns considered not only by reading peers but illumined and extended by the points of view and presentation of Jane Austen, George Eliot, Voltaire, Marcel Proust, Jean Paul Sartre or Albert Camus and granted their wisdom and perspective.

That participants in our reading group consider themselves intellectually and socially at home with their fellow readers was convincingly illustrated at a "special" summer meeting in a mountain cabin called just to touch base and to share a potluck lunch. One reader had lost her husband a week before, but she came, knowing, as she put it, that in this group she would "be as safe as anywhere," a statement that touched and honored us all.

In a different group, Mary attended a summer meeting arranged by her fellow readers to wish her farewell as she and her husband were moving to closer proximity with their children. To her surprise, she found the room decorated for Christmas. As Mary wondered at the decors, she was reminded that the previous Christmas she had mistaken the date for a reader meeting and come for lunch where no lunch was held. To bid her good speed, her friends celebrated her with a Christmas luncheon on a hot summer's day; a practical joke lovingly played which eased Mary's departure for her and the others as well.

A good reading group may serve yet another function, namely as an imaginary audience for writing projects we may want to undertake. It may happen that if we learn to love reading, we become passionate about writing as well. How many of us wish our mothers or grandmothers had nourished such a passion and written down a book of days: a description of special events in their lives, stressful and joyous, their difficulties of adjusting to single or married lives and the joys of togetherness when things went well, sporadic observations about husbands and children, friends and relatives, anything to bring them closer and deepen our understanding and appreciation. Writing journals or memoirs for ourselves or our children takes no special talent, only overcoming the feeling of its potential lack as well as our general inertia.

Proof of that assertion may be found in "inspirational" stories everywhere, such as that of the 88-year-old retired Washington farmer, who wrote his life history in sixty-eight pages. The newspaper article celebrating his achievement stated that "Geroux started writing—longhand, in his Brownstown workshop, sitting between a card table and his red 1942 Farmall Model H International tractor—[not telling anyone except his wife] what he was doing. [This] great-grandfather who didn't go to high school just sat and wrote—and wrote and wrote and wrote. He didn't read a how-to book or take a writing class. He did it the way he did other things: By just doing it."

The recipients of the finished work, his children and grandchildren, received their Christmas gift, a typewritten brown spiral notebook, with gratitude and awe. "I couldn't put it down, not even for a second," said one of his granddaughters. "It was just the best gift, his story, written down like that." She proudly displays the book on her coffee table. Another keeps her copy on a bookshelf "alongside biographies of American presidents. 'To me, this is the story of another very important life,'" she commented. "It is really a story of dealing with how the cards are dealt to you."

If writing books or journals seems too arduous a task or too strenuous a beginning, making scrapbooks is within anyone's ability and offers as many approaches as there are minds and hands. Scrapbooks come in different guises. Their common denominator is celebration and remembrance.

One such, lovingly made of scraps—pictures, cards, notes, pieces of fabrics, hand prints of children—aimed to catch the fleeing memory of a mother who was losing herself to Alzheimer's. It was produced by a woman in a scrapbook class we attended. She cut old photos into shapes fitting the accompanying narrative of people and events. About a dozen pages capture her mother's early years, parents and siblings, school, marriage, children, working years, special vacations, and grandchildren. An additional page for each of her children's families rounds out the history. Word has it Mother loves her memory book and looks at it every day. Of all the scrapbooks we made, that one was the most touching. It released in us all the wellspring of a need everyone shares, to remember and be remembered.

Another kind of scrapbook was assembled by free-lance writer Lynn Murray Willeford a month before her son Brook graduated from college. She "shook a mess of stained, wrinkled clippings and odd-sized pieces of paper from the cookbooks in [her] kitchen and set to work on his graduation present. 'I meant to put together a book of recipes that would remind him of home—our family home—as he moved off into a world of his own.'"

Written out in neat longhand, the book is less a book of "scraps" than one created from scraps into a unified whole. Even so, a scrapbook is a book of remembrance. Cooking the foods of his childhood, Brook is preserving his memories in the process.

"When he cooks Gallo Pinto or Senora Silvia's Chicken Salsa, he will remember his months in the cloud-forest of Santa Elena. The faces of his old island neighbors will pop up when he whips up Richard's Potatoes, Shirlee's Never-Fail Pie Crust or Cheryl's White-Lightning Chili. He will think of his dad and me when he follows our recipes for 'inis' (scaloppini), or chicken curry. Instructions for second-cousin Mado's brandy-heavy French pot roast, Nana's margaritas and Aunt Laurie's fried dodies keep alive relatives long gone and connect him to those still with us." Brook took the book with him clear across the country to his life in Boston.

Real food is different from take-out and even pizza home delivery, both of which we treat with increasing casualness. Leaving food on our plates has become habitual in the last two generations as our children and grandchildren imbibe and ingest commercially produced or "fast" foodstuff. Eating those, they have lost awareness of the relationship between the meat and potatoes on their plates and the work of hands and minds that went into producing, cooking, and getting them there. Pellegrini would say they have missed the opportunity to acquire gratitude for the good things of the earth.

Good homemade food has depth; it reveals a story about the mind that conceives it and the hands that make it; and it invites respect for those efforts. This was brought home one summer when a troop of twenty-six-year-old actors, cameramen and technicians descended on Inga's house for a month in the process of making a movie, the project of her actor son. Operating on a shoestring, they had budgeted for only one meal a day to be provided by an outside vendor, so Inga cooked. Fifty pounds of flour, meat from the store and volunteered neighborhood freezers, and vegetables from everyone's garden made up the dinners served buffet style or around the dinner table, depending on the number of eaters, which varied from day to day, depending on who was on set and who was not. Often the young diners would comment on the food and ask, "how come it tastes so deep?" Used to picking up food at fast food places, the encounter of their palates with those just picked vegetables, bread from the oven, and meat off the grill "rocked" them. They ate food history with their meals.

They liked everything, but among their favorite dishes were *Beef Burgundy* and *Leem's Chicken*, followed by either *Chocolate Layer Cake* or *Summer Tart.*

Beef Burgundy for a Crowd

Originally a recipe exchanged among graduate students at the University of Washington, it has now become an example of "free hand" cooking. We can list ingredients but the amounts vary with the size of the crowd.

Buy a full cut of round steak about ½ inch thick.
Have on hand:
Onions and garlic to taste
1 bottle of red wine
Beef broth
Fresh or canned mushrooms
Olive oil for braising the meat
Salt and pepper for seasoning.
Flour for thickening the sauce.

Cut meat into squares large enough to necessitate eating with a knife and fork. (This is not a stew). Brown sliced onions and garlic. Remove from pan and add enough oil to braise the meat squares. When all are browned, add onion, garlic, red wine and beef broth to cover the meat and let the mixture simmer till meat is tender. During the last part of the cooking, add fresh or canned mushrooms. Thicken slightly and serve on rice.

Leem's Chicken

This recipe was passed on from a friend who brought it from California. It is a dish both children and adults enjoy. It must be prepared a day before serving, which makes it convenient to stick in the oven on the night of a party.

4 lbs. chicken boiled with celery, onion and bay leaf
    and cut from bones
1 doz. corn tortillas cut into 1-inch strips
1 can mushroom soup
1 can cream of chicken soup
1 cup milk
1 grated onion
2 cans green chili salsa
1 lb. of grated sharp cheddar

In large pan put one layer of tortillas and one of chicken; repeat. Pour over this the rest of the ingredients, mixed. Put grated cheese on top. Let stand overnight. Bake about 1½ hours at 300 degrees. Cheese should be completely melted and slightly bubbling. Let stand a few minutes before serving.

Dinners such as these are perfect occasions for jug wines. We tried several. Everyone liked the Gato Negro Merlot and Chardonnay from Chile. They are hardy wines as are the slightly more expensive Robert Mondavi Woodbridge Merlot and Pinot Grigio. All come in half gallons. At the least expensive end is Gallo's Hearty Burgundy or Café Chardonnay, which like the others have good, strong varietal flavors and go well with the hearty dishes we served. A more recent possibility is Charles Shaw's "Two Buck Chuck" which varies from bottle to bottle, but at that price no one can expect sustained quality in every lot.

The chocolate cake the young movie crew liked is one that can be made any time and will get better with each day till on the last day, the last bite tastes best of all. Inga brought back the recipe from her village in Denmark, where in her childhood, weddings, christenings, confirmations and "round" birthdays were rituals to be celebrated in different stages. Following the initial festivity to which only relatives and close friends would be invited were one or more "afternoon coffees" honoring the women of families who had sent flowers or presents to the celebrant whom they knew, but to whom they were more distantly related than the guests at the original celebration. These coffee gatherings featured a dozen different cakes and cookies and warranted frequent recipe exchanges. The chocolate cake made it across the ocean because it is not only very good, but because it will take on any flavor the baker desires by leaving out the cocoa and exchanging the cup of strong coffee for one of rum, whiskey, or fresh lemon juice. It is thus a pound cake for all occasions and tastes.

Mrs. B's Chocolate Cake With or Without Custard

5 large eggs
2 1/3 cups of sugar
½ pound of margarine
1 2/3 cups of flour
1 t. baking powder
1 cup strong, cold coffee
2-4 T. unsweetened cocoa

Cream margarine with sugar. Beat in eggs. Add remaining ingredients. Bake either in two loaf pans (in which case an addition of almonds or walnuts is a good idea) or in two spring forms. Bake at 300 degrees till done, approximately one hour, depending somewhat on the shape of the baking tins. Cool.

If you choose to use the spring forms, cut each round cake horizontally and put custard (same recipe as in Chapter Two) between the four layers. Frost with dark but not unsweetened chocolate dissolved in a small pan with some whipping cream.

Summer Tart uses the same crust as the one used for *Apricot Tart* in Chapter Two, but the filling is different and the pie shell is baked for about fifteen to twenty minutes at 325 degrees and cooled before the filling is added.

Summer Tart

Make and bake piecrust as shown in Chapter Two

For Lemon Cream:
4 large egg yolks
12 T. sugar
4 t. lemon juice
¼ cup butter

Stir together all four ingredients and cook over medium heat till mixture thickens. Cool. Spoon into piecrust and arrange fresh raspberries or sliced peaches on top. Serve with a topping of whipped cream, or pass a bowl for individual indulgence.

It is a great pleasure to watch young people eat and to share in their events of the day. We experienced a sense of community in our house that season of movie making as all of us worked, in accordance with individual talent and skills, toward a common goal. Some participants indulged a summer passion which faded with fall and winter chills. Others are still pursuing careers in the movie world as actors, directors, writers or technicians. At no time in our lives can we know when we start a project, if the passion that fuels it is ethereal like summer wine or will endure through autumn and beyond.

The important thing, as we know from experience, is to find a place to begin. If we cannot conceive or do not dare initiate a long term project because we are not sure we can really commit to it or that it will sustain our interest, perhaps it is not a bad idea to start with a series of smaller ones.

Among our respondents, a woman who "loved doing newspaper work" found that volunteering to do newsletters for the organizations to which she belongs is "a modified version of the same," demanding less sustained time and energy but giving a measure of satisfaction nonetheless.

If we are ready, however, to launch into a memoir or other sustained writing projects, help and encouragement may be found in books and classes. Frequently peer groups are available for the asking, especially in metropolitan areas. Jill, who graduated from the Iowa School of Writing and teaches creative writing in college, says that belonging to a group of writers critiquing one another's work can be very rewarding if the rules for such participation are laid down from the start and individual writers agree to abide by them.

One rule at Iowa, she pointed out, is that the writer whose work is being critiqued is barred from speaking during the entire session. She is supposed to take notes, study them and on reflection decide to make changes in the manuscript in accordance with her own assessment of the comments and their validity. As a matter of course, all participants are expected to give as much as they take. Studied, helpful comments on the manuscripts of other writers are the currency for buying similar responses to one's own work. Final authority rests in the teacher whose experience and expertise are granted by all.

Such authority is lacking in more informal peer writing groups, Jill pointed out. In that setting, the writer's ego may get in the way of listening to the readers and actually absorbing the stated differences between what the readers see and what the writer wants them to see, which in turn produces a clash between the writer's desire to hear "I like it just the way it is" and the voices of reality that point out failures of communication due to shortcomings of either content or style.

Writing is a part of the writer. It takes courage and confidence to separate one from the other and benefit from a critique of the former, but given those, Jill emphasized, a group of fellow writers may offer invaluable help and encouragement.

We should note in this context that if our egos are not up to the critique offered by fellow writers or critics whom we pay for such service, an alternative is writing for ourselves, as many have done who have written memoirs not so much for publication as for an initial step into the world of writers and shared evaluations.

"I've come to understand, " writes Diane Howitz in *Women Confronting Retirement*, "that revisiting the past through writing may be a bridge between my working life and my life to come. Perhaps being mired in the past isn't totally self-indulgent, purely sentimental, or a substitute for action; it may signify an active engagement with the present. Now and then I feel that I am trying on a new identity, searching for a writing voice and the confidence to bring ideas and stories dancing in my mind to light ... Mostly I read books about writing, or become immersed in other people's essays, anything to avoid writing myself. But I find I am reading with a new eye." Howitz has discovered that if writing only improves our reading as piano lessons enhance our appreciation of a professional pianist's playing, we have enriched our lives forever with a taste of the inexhaustible values of literary and artistic performance—as audience as well as performers.

A passion for reading may not necessarily lead to writing, of course. Donna, who taught college English for twenty-seven years, became a storyteller. She uses her skills of text analysis and interpretation to present programs of Texas lore before groups and conventioneers. Doing that, she says, gives her even greater satisfaction than teaching, which she loved. Others are prompted to learn new languages or move in an entirely different direction. A retired physician we know read *Gods and Generals* and *Killer Angels* on a friend's enthusiastic recommendation. She is now an inveterate Civil War buff, studying and visiting battlefields and reading up on documents and scholarly works. Her initially small investment of time led to a much larger engagement along entirely unexpected lines.

Moving to a different realm, the out-of-doors, we found that everyone—city women and country dwellers alike—who responded to our questionnaire mentioned gardening in her answer to our question of how to spend time profitably. Many reported that their gardens had been primary beneficiaries of their retirement time, rewarding them with unparalleled bloom. For some it was a passion to be shared, a way to initiate social relationships and events, such as annual garden tours. Some combined learning and teaching about gardening by signing up for a Washington State sponsored program entitled "Master Gardeners." Participants attended classes one day a week for approximately four months and then volunteered for answering the phone in the garden center office where people call in with questions about soil, flowers, or vegetables—about two thousand calls a year. Their weekly column in the local newspaper provides further stimulation for educating both writers and readers and creating a "garden community."

To the social benefits of growing a garden may be added the psychological advantages which have been outlined in a series of studies made by Stephen Kaplan of the University of Michigan. "Those who look after the ill and elderly get less tired if they walk or cycle through greenery," he claims. Cancer patients "go back to work sooner after treatment if they walk in natural surroundings or gardens; tenants in bad housing show less aggression and violence if their flats overlook something natural; girls with greener views from home are more self-disciplined and concentrate better."

This is hardly new information if we consider that the Victorians built public gardens because they thought the poor would behave better and enjoy better health if they had ready access to greenery. Yet Kaplan's claims are timely, as we consider the generation of baby-boomers reaching middle age and retirement, a time in their lives when their enthusiasm for gardening, latent or new, allegedly will reach a peak.

We were especially heartened by this enthusiasm for gardening in varying forms and degrees expressed by all respondents to our questionnaires as it tempered our reading of Alicia Skinner Cook's article from 1991 "Comparison of Leisure Patterns and Morale between Retired Professional and Nonprofessional Women." Cook concludes that "professional women had higher rates of participation in spectator art activities and spectator sports, participation in elections and political activities, participation in organizations, traveling and going to parties," whereas nonprofessional women exceeded their professional cohorts only in "gardening and/or care of animals and plants, and being with children and grandchildren." Perhaps professional women are catching up on their gardening skills—to their greater satisfaction and benefit.

Cook furthermore notes that the three activities "rated highest in terms of frequency of participation" were the same for both groups of women: reading, being with neighbors and friends, and watching television or listening to the radio, albeit different programs. Whatever the validity of her findings, and however they may relate to the world of today, Cook's study warrants our attention as one of the first attempts to compare women to women rather than offer the standard comparison of women to men; a comparison which should always be considered with due attention to the differences between the two groups in the way of professional and social conditions determining their lives both before and after retirement. Women's work history differs from men's, in terms of longevity and interruptions; and men's social position before and after retirement differs from women's. Men are, for example, given license to marry younger mates as women are not, and they do, but women are more skilled in developing relationships with other women, behaviors which influence the lives of the two sexes differently.

In addition to gardening, tennis and especially golf appeared as favored activities among our questionnaire respondents, some of whom continued playing right into their eighties and beyond. One, who at eighty-three plays tennis on a regular basis emphasized the joy of participating with others at whatever level she can manage on a given day. Another, who never before engaged in athletic activities, finds that in her retirement she can enjoy golf three times a week even with the realization that she will never perform as she might had she started young. New to a retirement village in Arizona, she signed up for membership in the local country club and now cherishes not only the golfing exercise but also the social encounters that go with it.

Games as a social activity offer the opportunity to lose ourselves in play as we did when we were children. In her essay
"Retiring Into Intensity, Experiencing 'Deep Play'," Barbara Fey
Waxman points out the biological and cultural advantages found in
the temporary absorption in an activity that allows us to forget
about ourselves in the course of its performance. "I love the
unambiguous, perfect structure of the tennis court, the clear rules
of play and fast motion of the ball; I am challenged to perform
backhand strokes or overheads, to get my serves in the right place
in the opponent's service box, to meet my opponent's challenging
returns, and to make the right choices from the overall menu of
winning strategies. When I am immersed in the flow of a match,
my mental and physical skills are honed and keenly focused. Win
or lose, I emerge from this play a rejuvenated person. At my age,
play may be a significant pathway to good health and happiness."
A clear signal, that for her, and haply for most of us, winning or
losing is not the central part of the activity; being revitalized is.
That is the spiritual dimension reward for a mature evaluation of
participation in whatever game we pursue.

The joys of tennis and golf notwithstanding, the tenor of
responses elicited by our questionnaire made us conclude that
hiking and its milder relative, walking, are predominant in the
realm of exercise. Walking can be done anywhere, on city streets
and in rural lanes, and more and more women of all ages have
discovered that finding one or more walking companions stimulates
our commitment to steady trudging, especially on inclement days
when it is all too easy to convince ourselves we can "skip today."
Talking along the way helps, and talk comes easily as we walk; it
falls into the rhythm of our footfalls as news is exchanged and
made open to speculation.

Some women form their own hiking groups for year round
venturing into the hills or countryside on foot, snow shoes or cross
country skis. Outings are arranged by all or by whoever volunteers
to take charge of disseminating information about proposed
destinations, time and meeting place. For such informal groups, e-
mail has proved an unexpected boon, replacing time consuming

phone calls otherwise needed to get everyone to the same destination at the same time.

Newcomers to a community or women who do not know other hikers or walkers may for a small fee join local organizations offering hiking, biking and ski outings. Our local *Cascadians* post offerings for any level of participation, as do *The Hard Core Runners* with their motto of "start slow and taper off." Among Cascadians, "The Pokies" meet weekly to do hikes of four miles with modest elevation, whereas the "Tuesday Hikers," also a weekly group, advertise hikes of upper-easy to advanced levels.

Participation in such groups offers physical, mental, and social stimulation as well as emotional support. Companionship eases the potential boredom of long stretches and lifts the fatigue of the last miles home. As importantly, group walks offer a feeling of safety in numbers and the leadership provided by the hiker who knows where she is going and how to get there.

The woman who responded to our questionnaire with a paragraph on hiking said she found her satisfaction at being able to move through the landscape at any pace reflected in other hikers. Although they were in the slower battalion of the hiking brigade, they knew they were lucky to be there at all. More and more, that dimension of gratitude at being on the street, the road, the mountain path, the course or the court—at all—becomes dominant as a determiner of our satisfaction.

We all like to perform well; we all like to "win," but at this time in our lives, we know that neither is as important as being players. As an exercise in developing gratitude and spiritual dimension, hiking in the mountains is exhilarating and for some as good as a churching. There, wide vistas, mountain peaks and craggy rocks with grand or scruffy pines, hemlock, and cedar speak the strong, stern language of permanence to their prodigal sisters, the flowers of the meadows, which squander their splendor all season long from grass widows and yellow bells to lupine, monkey flower, asters and late summer's gentian. The flowers pay no attention because they know that their strength is in change as they die and come back with every recurrent season. Both they and their solemn brothers are there for us to see and will be there when we can see no longer. All of them live without our taking any responsibility for either their presence or continuance beyond the respectful treatment we owe all nature's creatures.

For those who live without ready access to mountains or countryside, Chet Raymo's *The Path: A One-Mile Walk Through the Universe* may show the way to outdoor exhilaration in its demonstration that a modest walk anywhere may awaken our senses to wonders equaling those of mountains and meadows. Raymo moved from Utah to Boston, from "great expanses of nature and of sparsely populated landscapes" to a city where population density "was more than 8,000 times that of Moab." Narrowing his field of vision and teaching himself to see the smaller wonders, he wrote a book which covers only one mile of ground, his daily walk to his teaching job at Stonehill College. It attests to his realization that even small spaces in crowded cities can yield worthwhile outdoor experiences and inexhaustible opportunities for "new knowledge and joy."

A reviewer of his book calls it a work of "patience and place, of the small pieces that combine to help one understand the larger world," and he quotes Raymo's conviction that, "A minute lived attentively can contain a millennium; and an adequate step can span the planet." All any of us have to do, wherever we are, is take the time to look and wonder, walk if we can, but most importantly, be present.

We also heard from women who can no longer be physically active beyond performing day-to-day tasks but who have found satisfaction in learning to become good audiences. They have developed social contacts by attending baseball, football, hockey, or tennis matches together with friends, followed perhaps with discussions over lunches or dinners which may take as a point of departure the shared sports event.

Our friend Sarah, who died shortly after her hundredth birthday, enjoyed watching the Mariners till the end. By then television had become her only venue, but she never missed a game. She recognized each player by name and number and knew his individual strengths and weaknesses. She had dealt herself into their world and made it hers.

We may hope that women like Sarah share May Sarton's insight that "the soul is a lithe and serene athlete" for in her enduring passion for the game and the players, which has bought her access to their "language," she is burning the light, the "radiant powers" of the Holy Ghost, which are inexhaustible.

Our "radiant powers"—born of living in the world with all our might and even as audiences seeing ourselves as part of creative forces at play—may be exercised in any kind of event or audience of which we are a part; in the world of sports as well as in that of art, theater, film, opera or ballet. All of those offer possibilities for not only individual enjoyment but for pleasures shared with friends either locally, nationally or abroad. Sharing artistic events inevitably fuels and focuses the discussions that are likely to follow.

That truth has long ago caught up with Elderhostel organizers who arrange tours all over the world with emphasis on music, art or history. The reason their lectures yield such general satisfaction among participants is the focus they provide as they inform in conjunction with artistic performances and thereby create context for both. A lecture on Mozart accompanied with a field trip to Mozart's house preceding a Mozart piano program in Salzburg is likely to make our responsive chords vibrate to much higher frequencies than would any one of the three events enjoyed by itself.

Social contacts in a group like that are readily established because the group is self selected. Each member signed up because she wanted to learn about music generally and Mozart specifically. Most importantly, individual participants are pursuing activities which at some level are in congruence with their interests and selves. That differentiates the traveler/pilgrim from the mere tourist.

Even greater enjoyment than that offered by the triple activity is experienced by those who can play an instrument and are therefore able to evaluate the performance at a level non players, with some exceptions of course, are less likely to reach. That alone should encourage and justify anyone's attempt at artistic endeavors be they good, bad, or indifferent. One of our questionnaire respondents signed up for a class in watercolor on just that premise.

She quickly realized she would never be a "master," but she found satisfaction through trial and error and developed a keener eye for the work of other water colorists.

Nor does she make apologies for her work. Year after year, she has her water colors reproduced as Christmas cards sent to friends who can in that way follow her development and be pleased for her. She looks forward to annual gallery hopping with friends or classmates and enjoys assisting with local art sales. The classes she takes have students of all ages which gives her the additional advantage of meeting people with different outlooks on life. One of our respondents was emphatic on that point, "it is important to participate in activities that include all ages, not just seniors," she wrote. She is seconded by another who tells a story of getting together with a group of women, all ages, every Saturday morning to learn new songs and sing together for the pleasure of all.

Because we are an enterprising culture, many of the activities we have discussed prove to have in them a business potential as well for women inclined to re-enter the marketplace where social intercourse is a given. Shanon Hicks in Pateros, Washington is putting her children through school, "stitch by stitch." Retired from a job as a dental assistant, she has made a business of doing custom quilt stitching for quilters around the country. Because she loves her work and wants to share her joy in doing it, Shanon also offers workshops in longarm machine quilting, a craft which only recently has gained recognition as an art form. In fact, Hicks was selected as a finalist in the national competition sponsored by *The Professional Quilter*, the first inclusion of a machine quilter in seventeen years.

Shanon's quilting career started seven years ago when she saw a demonstration of the longarm machine. She had sewing in her genes passed on from her mother and grandmother who sewed and quilted, but the longarm really turned her on at a time in her life when she had tired of her job and wanted a career without end. She invested in a machine and has been quilting ever since, challenging herself to learn new ways by signing up as a student in the annual quilters' conference in Redmond.

Equally successful but skeptical about the value of classes is Susan Gruner of *Russell's Draperies*. "If you want to go deeper, you have to do it yourself," she says—and does. Confessing to a lifelong love of sewing, she researched the topic as an art form and eventually focused on that of drapery during the seventeenth, eighteenth, and nineteenth centuries when it was practiced by skilled drapers using compasses and plumb lines. Gruner, too, uses compasses and plumb lines in the work she does independently or in liaison with home decorators in the town where she lives. Her sewing machines she bought from a retired draper in Roy, Washington who had advertised them for sale through the *Society for Creative Anachronism*. She wonders at her success and is never in want of customers. But, she says, "it's the challenge that keeps me interested."

Likewise, the challenge to learn something new started a retired biologist and amateur weaver making calendars featuring the year in her hometown and environs. Already a trained photographer, Amanda took computer courses in imaging and "photo shop" and was eventually able to take and arrange pictures into beautiful calendar pages providing valuable records of more than days for the local population.

A purely altruistic attempt at invoking business for a project fuelled by passion is Olga Bloom's success at renovating an old coffee barge into a floating concert hall. A retired concert pianist, she staked her mortgage on the purchase and renovation of the boat so that talented but unknown chamber musicians might perform in it and make "Bargemusic," twice a week. They get a chance to do creative work, and audiences like the reasonable ticket prices to the "wood paneled hall" where four picture windows feature the Manhattan skyline. Olga Bloom gets her payment in the coin of music, which for her constitutes the good life.

Finally, Oprah's example has taught us that even book clubs may take on the aura of selling agents. We described above the workings of a somewhat academic—and in this context, staid—reading group, but such organizations come in all guises responding to the needs of individual and collective members. *The Pulpwood Queens* of Jefferson, Texas drink pineapple champagne punch and wear matching pink T-shirts, leopard-skin-print shoes, signature tiaras and rhinestone pins for their meetings in the "Beauty and the Book," Kathy Patrick's bookstore cum beauty parlor.

This group is not just any old book club. It carries some freight. Last June they kicked off *Good Morning America's* "Read This Book Club," and their choice of *The Dive from Clausen's Pier* allegedly sent sales skyrocketing. They are a marketing force, a book group franchise. "Six locals, " according to one reviewer, "have in the past year grown to almost 300, with 13 chapters across Texas and Louisiana ... What is happening here, quietly in Jefferson, Texas, population 2,100, is the collision, and collusion, of several potent cultural forces at work in the combustible publishing industry—regional color and national mega-marketing, plain-folks intimacy with an eye on the camera. But mostly, it's proof that even amid our high-tech, mondo-corporate culture, the little guy can still get a piece of the action. All it takes is a little ingenuity and a lot of moxie ... Many mid-or low-list authors now automatically create Web sites devoted to their books, do phone interviews with book groups around the country, and generally throw themselves at the public like an alchemist tossing powders on a flame, hoping for the magical explosion."

Our goal is to promote literacy, claims Kathy Patrick, to have some fun besides, and, we may add, amidst their potluck fare of coconut coated chicken skewers and spicy hamburger casseroles to sniff a scent of business in the air.

That book groups are taken seriously as major players in the book buying business is furthermore shown by "the list of questions for reading groups" appended more and more contemporary works. Even a serious book like *Crabwalk*, which details the sinking of the German refugee carrier "Wilhelm Gustloff" by a Soviet submarine in 1945, features on the inside jacket, a good inch below the picture of the author, Gunter Grass, 1999 Nobel Prize Winner for Literature, a "Reading Group Guide available at www.HarcourtBooks.com."

An "intellectual" book, one of the few that addresses the extensive suffering of the German civilian population from 1943 onward and published by a major house, acknowledges in its list of questions the market potential among book group buyers. Some good might come of that along the line of raising our national discourse.

A plethora of opportunities are revealed in these examples. Do we have the ingenuity and the moxie to catch them on the wing?

4

FROM PROFESSIONAL
PROMPTS TO SELF-GENERATED
CHALLENGE

The category [of women] ... worth its weight in gold,
contains those women of character who haven't neglected to enrich their minds and are capable of creating
a life of their own when nature begins to desert them;
these women are determined to decorate their minds,
just as earlier they have decorated their faces ... They
replace physical attraction by an engaging kindness as
well as by a sprightliness which grows all the more
charming with age; in this way they somehow manage
to come closer to being young by winning the affection
of the young.

— *Dangerous Liaisons*, 1782

If you bring forth what is within you, it will save you. If
you do not bring forth what is within you, it will kill
you.

— *The Gospel of Thomas*

As we initiate retirement, professional women are mentally
alive and alert. We have met and responded to the challenges of our careers, and we are concerned about their lack in

retirement because our psychological well-being and sense of vitality have become linked with challenge and response.

One hundred percent of the women answering our questionnaires noted that they had "greatly" enjoyed professional challenges during their working careers, and sixty-eight percent admitted to missing them in retirement. The remaining thirty-two percent had found ways to transform the mental stimulation yielded by their careers into intellectual challenge in their Third Stage.

The sixty-eight percent notwithstanding, all reported they are busy—and yet they feel something is missing. What that may be is yet a topic for present and future scholarly research notes Christine Ann Price in her book from 1998 on *Women and Retirement: the Unexplored Transition.* No one so far, she says, has studied that domain. Price's target group is professional women, who have admitted to missing the challenge offered by their former professions. "No longer did they encounter various problems, novel experiences, or puzzling dilemmas on a daily basis. Although most of the women became involved in a variety of activities which required thoughtful consideration and practical skills, many felt an initial longing for the challenges they formerly confronted."

One of the women she interviewed regretted missing "some of the challenge, you know, being able to help [somebody] out, to figure out a problem ... you miss that." Another woman in Price's study addresses specifically the absence of long-term goals as she acknowledges her envy of a former colleague who is still working and who talks about a new direction in her life. "I almost feel envious," she comments, because suddenly I just ... realize I don't have any long-term goals anymore ... I don't know, it's a different feeling. And I thought this ... this is kind of crazy 'cause it's not from boredom or lack of something to do. I can't look forward to another career, don't want to ... don't want to ... And yet, if you don't have some kind of goal, ah, I'm beginning to feel kind of ... empty is certainly not the right word because I am very much involved in things I like to do. But somehow there's not a sense of direction that I used to feel." Clearly, being busy is in itself not enough. If we don't know what we are being busy about and where our business is taking us, we perceive something missing.

Our culture promotes "busyness," double or triple scheduling, and crowded calendars. They are signs of our being successful and useful to the world, and, as such, characteristic of our career lives. By staying busy in the Third Stage we resemble ourselves in the Second Stage and thereby keep old age at bay. Yet as Margaret Cruikshank observes in her book *Learning to Be Old*, if we want to believe that the old "are intrinsically worthy or that life beyond wage earning is intrinsically good," we cannot cling to the belief that busyness is "redemptive." Busyness is a utilitarian value and perhaps an unimaginative expectation to harbor for people in late life.

We have throughout accepted Friedan's "fountain" of age as a wellspring of encouragement for mature people to seek adventure and model generativity in their advancing years. At the same time, we should not close our ears to Harry Moody's admonition that society's ideal of productivity may "ensnare and defeat us" when we are no longer able or interested in "producing." "We need a wider vision of what late-life productivity may mean," he argues in "Age, Productivity, and Transcendence," a "vision that includes values such as altruism, citizenship, creativity, and the search for faith." Accepting constructive busyness as an objective should therefore not allow us to overlook the possibility that old age has meanings not shared with mid-life; nor should we necessarily accept the pragmatic view held by some gerontologists which de-emphasizes the possibilities of late-life spiritual development.

In contrast, we applaud the potential of "spiritual" development and add to that kind of growth mental challenge and stimulation. We furthermore venture that the emptiness experienced by the professional women in Price's study and implied in the responses we received—the lack of direction despite involvement in things we like to do—resides in the difference between the professional and the self generated challenge. The former is contextual—stated and perceived within the terms of a given profession—and legitimized by the purpose it serves; whereas the latter is contextual only to the extent we have generated a context of our world and ourselves in it and legitimized solely as serving the process toward our becoming fully integrated, authentic human beings living the lives we consider good and useful to ourselves and others.

It runs counter to our Puritan prescription of busyness to contextualize and legitimize our self designed undertakings because they smack of self-indulgence. The self-instigated task is one that does not *have to* be done and therefore should not be accorded value. Yet, now as before, we want the gratification we experienced when in our careers we gave full attention to a task. We felt useful then as we temporarily forgot about ourselves. Now the task is of our own making, and we must therefore re-learn the capacity for absorption in work as in play which we experienced so readily when we were children and practiced in our career lives as well.

To be subsumed in our tasks, letting ourselves be one with the activity, is to experience the flush of personal integrity which Erik Erikson contends is necessary to encounter the despair of old age. Erikson's image of the fully mature person is someone who acknowledges and contains the less than ideal world in which we live and sees her own life in it as fulfilling a design of her own making. For that design there is no blueprint. It is the figure in the carpet of our true selves in the context of our living in the world. Ferreting out that figure even as we draw it is our existential conundrum and mandate. We must risk letting go of ourselves to find ourselves in the carrying out of an activity in whatever realm, at whatever level, in the intensity of a tennis game, the meting out of seeds in a garden row, the writing of a text, the quilting of a bedspread, the creating of a dinner, whatever is truly the object of our attention, whatever completes our clearly or dimly perceived design.

Self designed context and self-appointed legitimacy furthermore demand self-created energy, yet another difference between workplace and home place. The synergy of the former, generated by several people joining energies to conceive and fuel a project, is missing as we start out by ourselves at our solitary writing desks, looms, pottery wheels, drafting boards or sewing machines relying on our own wills to drive the enterprise.

To arrive at Erikson's "wholeness and perspective," therefore, will require not only our willing it and wanting it but our learning and practicing ways to achieve it. Success in that endeavor will to some extent depend on our aptitude for lateral—out of the box—thinking. Meeting professional challenges, we exercised a great deal of vertical thinking and occasionally demonstrated lateral thinking as well. As we worked with colleagues to conceive and formulate responses to a given challenge—an improved system for evaluating student work, for example—we would consider what we had done so far, lay out the steps we had taken, gauge successes and failures and try to imagine the next step. In short, we would think vertically, begin by making assumptions based on past experience and proceed from those. In this case, we might decide to re-write the rubrics we had used, making them more or less specific, simpler or more complex, or re-evaluate our grading procedures.

Relying on vertical thinking, we may make those minor changes, or we might break new ground using lateral thinking, seeing the problem from a different perspective, and arrive at the realization that neither grades nor rubrics are the fairest or best ways of evaluating student performance. A teacher's written assessment paired with the student's self-evaluation, for instance, might give a clearer, more inclusive impression of both work and effort expended.

Because it is not based on past assumptions about what works and what does not, lateral thinking has a lower "probability" rating than vertical thinking, which operates within expected and therefore more clearly defined outcomes. The resulting solution, therefore, may be a great success or a dismal failure demanding more evaluation and yet another approach. Lateral thinking means taking risks in hopes of higher yields.

Creating and meeting challenges in our retirement lives demand some lateral thinking because neither the context—the profession—nor the purpose—the need to generate or improve existing programs or strategies—is a given. Both must be self generated and depend for their existence on the amount of self knowledge we have acquired in the living of our lives as well as the knowledge we are gaining as we set and meet challenges in retirement. This means that the projects we undertake teach us who we are even as we choose them in accordance with that knowledge. We build the road as we walk it.

Uncovering new perspectives, practicing lateral thinking, we may proceed in a number of different ways. We may doodle, or sketch or make lists enumerating strengths and weaknesses, desirable goals or undertakings, to help us find what we want to discover and to offer a sign of the direction to take as well as an estimation of our fitness for the endeavor. Merle Geline Rubine's contribution to *Women Confronting Retirement* outlines the route she took toward finding a direction for her retirement life. A "personal inventory" revealed she had "excellent health, no dependents, management skills, intellectual curiosity, wanderlust, a sense of humor, a youthful spirit, an apartment that could generate income." She lacked "strong computer skills, a second or third language, a master's degree, status as a media superstar or a top executive."

She had worries as well about "living outside the loop once [she] left the network [as a television news producer], being old and poor, forced by necessity to downsize [her] lifestyle, becoming bitter." She hoped to "connect with the world and make new commitments and to find a sense of use and purposefulness." Brave enough to add up the pluses and minuses, she was rewarded with the discovery that "what [she] lacked was less important than what [she] had" and the next step was to determine what she wanted to do. Second careers, she concluded, should be gifts to ourselves and not necessarily the product of reasonable or prudent choices—a bit of lateral versus vertical thinking. Another list ensued of things she most enjoyed: "researching and reporting stories, poking around in antiques stores and flea markets, traveling, making new friends, going to the ballet and theater." Enumeration of occupations relating to these favorite activities followed: "writer, reporter, specializing in issues of aging, antiques dealer, Peace Corps volunteer, character actress in television commercials." After careful evaluation of those choices, she eliminated everything but the Peace Corps. She had thought of signing up back in the sixties when her New York roommates had joined, but the time hadn't been right. Now it was, and she caught opportunity on the wing.

After her turn abroad, she came back to New York convinced that "joining the Peace Corps in Africa was overwhelmingly the best decision [she] had ever made for [herself]."

She acknowledges being scared when she left NBC. "I had grown accustomed to the perks and privileges of a high-status profession. There was the possibility that I would not find my way outside of the corporate world and I would have little to look forward to but getting old and feeling irrelevant. But my Peace Corps experience is giving me all that I had hoped to find: challenge, a sense of purpose, a sense of accomplishment, a great adventure, and a path to follow ... So I haven't retired. I am progressing, moving on, starting over."

Ms. Geline Rubin learned for herself that generating an idea for a solution to a problem, such as how to spend our post retirement lives in a satisfying, useful way, produces the chemical seretonin in the brain cells which encodes the idea and gives us the "high" we associate with feeling good. (Runners will know the feeling). While we are high on the idea and fully engaged in getting ready for an assignment in Africa, writing our memoirs, painting the view from our living room window, or piecing a quilt, we are mildly concerned about the outcome. Soon enough, however, we realize that not only is the process of living in a third world country, writing, painting, or piecing demanding in themselves, but the outcome remains doubtful throughout. In the process of carrying out our plan, therefore, we will reevaluate it, walk some flat stretches of road; but then with each success or epiphany, we will once again experience the serotonin flush. Or we may give up on our initial inspiration and hope for another to set us back on the road to accomplishment. Some women go through a series of stops and starts before they decide on one thing, but from each experience something will have been learned, and we must take it on faith that the aggregate of that learning will eventually ripen into a project worth being persistent about.

Women who think themselves deficient in stick-to-it-ness may gain some comfort from Albert Einstein's observation that "the mere formulation of a problem is far more essential than its solution, which may be merely a matter of mathematical or experimental skills. To raise new questions, new possibilities, to regard old problems from a new angle requires creative imagination and marks real advances in science." We will add to that, in the Humanities and in our lives as well.

The women who responded to our question of how they would find or had found ways to transform the mental stimulation of their careers to post retirement intellectual challenge did not offer specific strategies, but all mentioned "continued learning" as both end and means. "I have become a broadcaster at an alternate radio station," wrote Jackie, a former English teacher. "This provides plenty of challenges, frustrations, endless learning experiences and contacts with both the young and interesting individuals." A former attorney describes her post retirement work as a court appointed special advocate for abused children in similar terms, "difficult, frustrating, sometimes rewarding work."

Others speak of "setting goals," "avoiding ruts," "remaining open to new opportunities" and, again and again, "seeking and meeting challenges," entirely self generated or induced by acceptance of difficult assignments in areas of significance such as child advocacy, mentoring of student teachers, or promoting the arts in elementary schools whose budgets have foreclosed their teaching or application. The common threads weaving through the fabric of these answers are a quest for challenges, openness to new possibilities, and long-term commitment to both. They are the woof. The warp is a positive attitude, and on that we had full consensus. We heard not a single whimper or whine. Our respondents had set up their looms. They were ready to weave a future. And thirty-two percent had already made cloth.

As they went about their work, they had furthermore perceived, clearly or dimly, in each case differently, that loss of external expectations will make intellectual exploration both easier and more difficult. Easier because we will have to come up to the standards set by ourselves and therefore likely to be passionate about. More difficult because we tend to judge our own standards and performance more severely than we do those posed and executed by others. We may remain undaunted, however, because we have agreed that challenge is a useful dimension in the lives of all adults and remains so till we refuse to meet it, or senility catches up with us.

So let us assume that we take up the gauntlet, design our projects and accord them attention and commitment. Our tasks will be free of external expectations and the pressure they bring, but they will not be without tension because that lodges at the root of all intensely felt experience: tension between our hankering after the true and tried and our yearning to stretch our minds and skills as far as they may reach and then a little; tension between our desire for comfort, physical and mental, and our quest for exploration beyond comfort's zone; and tension between our excitement about a project and doubts about its outcome.

We risk failure with any new thing we try, but only those ventures we do *not* seek will have a one hundred percent failure rate. From almost any pursuit something is gleaned, something learned. As we enlarge our consciousness by learning and trying something new or giving full attention where before we dabbled, we may see our worlds in a different light or from a different perspective. "There seems to be a law," says Anne Truitt, "that the more conscious knowledge you develop, the more you can expand your consciousness. The artist takes advantage of this law. Wise artists like Titian and Rembrandt and Matisse became greater as they grew older." We may add to that other facts such as Verdi's composing *Othello* at seventy-one and *Falstaff* at eighty, Picasso still painting in his nineties, Grandma Moses first putting brush to canvas at seventy-six, and Immanual Kant writing his greatest philosophical works in his late fifties and sixties. They make a claim for the last stages in life, pronouncing them intrinsically good.

Most of us cannot come up to those standards, but we can learn for ourselves that given time for contemplation, we, too, can experience new insights, however modest, and even an occasional epiphany. If we resume work on a part time basis, we may readily identify with *Fortune's* list of ninety-year-olds still at work, ranging from doctors, lawyers, and CEOs to barbers and fry cookers. Contemporary scientific discoveries about the functioning of brains throughout our life spans give us additional hope of continued involvement and fulfillment. The *Journal of Rehabilita-*

tion Medicine from May 2003 records recent findings pertaining to regenerative potential—neurogenesis—of adult brains. Until recently, research found generation of neurons confined to a discrete developmental period, but lately exceptions have been located in several regions of the brain, "that have been shown to generate new neurons well into the post natal and adult period. One of the best-characterized regions is the sub granular zone of the dentate gyrus in the brain, where granule neurons are generated throughout life from a population of progenitor/stem cells. Furthermore, recent findings suggest that neurogenesis may be of importance to memory function as well as mood disorders." These findings raise for us the question that given lifelong potential of generation of neurons, the loss of which has heretofore been considered irreversible and the cause of neurological disease and impairment: how may we ourselves contribute to our personal neurogenesis?

We may engage in mind stimulating projects, and in addition we may make habits of solving crossword puzzles or playing computer software games or exercises, activities which to date have been demonstrated and validated by contemporary experts as means of improving brain wiring. Other studies have concluded that "elderly people who frequently read, play board games, play musical instruments, or dance several or more days per week have a lesser risk of developing dementia than those who rarely (once weekly or less frequently) participate in these leisure activities." Some or all of those pursuits are readily available to us and may be one of the ways we can seek the challenges which will enable us to stay mentally alive and, we may infer, generate neurons.

Other studies argue a link between mental and physical exercise. In *Women and Aging: Transcending the Myths*, Linda Gannon concludes that, "elderly people who are able and willing to remain active are less likely to show deficits, since these individuals continue to gain practice and experience. Because cultural demands and expectations may yield a 'self-fulfilling prophecy,' this information should be widely disseminated in order to dispel the myth of universal age-related cognitive deterioration." Gannnon's reference to "deficits" arises from her knowledge of longitudinal studies—comparisons of the same individuals throughout their life spans—which have found that "individuals remain on a stable course even during the critical periods of 67 to 74 years of age." However, "the cohort born later in the century (birth cohort) retained higher positions throughout a lifespan. The investigators observed that the differences found in cohort studies reflected variations stemming from non-age-related rapid technological-cultural changes, not from intrinsic (ontogenetic) decline." It is likely, then, to make the assumption that today's 70-year-olds compared to today's 30-year-olds will show a "cognitive deficit," but that this "deficit" is not necessarily related to age but to "differences in educational level and other relevant cultural factors." From those findings, we may further venture that as far as professional women are concerned, we may be among the fortunate ones who have experienced in our lives the "educational levels" and "cultural factors," which Gannon relates to diminished "cognitive deficit." If that is so, do we not have a mandate, a responsibility even, to lead the way to an understanding that life in the Third Stage may indeed be intrinsically good?

For us then, old age should be no excuse for indulging in untargeted "busyness" or for lacking willingness to explore, provide commitment to our self-assigned tasks, or fashion a serviceable attitude. Those are determiners for continued vitality and may be developed under any circumstances, no matter how dire, and no matter how "reduced" or shackled we may feel with advancing age and its corollary of decreasing status in the world. Women's prison literature bears eloquent testimony to that supposition.

Danish history tells of a woman who lost well nigh everything and built a world of the leavings. King's daughter and wife of his prime minister, she remained through all vicissitudes her own mind's mistress. Alleged complicity in her husband's treasonous dispositions against the Danish crown cost her twenty-two years of imprisonment in the stony Blue Tower adjoining the royal apartments in the castle of seventeenth century Copenhagen. Piece by piece she was deprived of her possessions until she stood naked before the queen's ladies-in-waiting who threw her some garments with which to cover her forty-two year old body. Her immediate challenge was to stave off cold and constipation, an ill matched pair of obstacles demanding contrasting treatment: remaining in bed was the most effective means to staying warm, but it subverted the need for motion to move her bowels. Yet they were moderate obstacles compared to the mental deprivations exerted against her. Her captors denied her privacy, fearing that she might put an end to her life. But she was wrought of tougher fibers. She made companions of sorts of the poor, illiterate, and sometimes criminal series of women who for a few annual coins were induced to share the former first lady's cell, six by seven paces. She could not hope to make them understand her forfeited world at the courts of Europe, but she could listen to their tales of life among the poor and in return teach them to read books, smuggled in by jailors she bribed with food from her plentiful prisoner's table. (Pride prevented the king, her half brother, to feed her less than royally). She could save her sugar wrappers, fashion a quill from a feather in her bedding and dip it in a combination of ale and soot, and with those implements set about to write a record of her prison experience. It is a narrative of liberation, inspiration even, and with it she solved the riddle of captivity, effected the balance of integrity and despair, which is labeled wisdom.

Twenty-two years of transforming physical and mental obstacles to challenges failed to diminish her spiritual, mental, or physical powers. She walked out her prison door "in style" as she put it, as tall and straight as she had entered.

Leonora's "retirement" was beyond negotiation as eventually all retirements are, no matter how many careers we may pursue, and her shrunken world, metaphorically speaking, is not so different in kind from that experienced by some professional women as we leave our employ. Countess Leonora Ulfeldt had fancied herself a somebody, and her world had supported her contention—not unlike the way professional women perceive their professional identity and status. In prison, she was reduced to simply "Leonora" and addressed no differently from the way the jailors spoke to her low life companions. Yet the woman in the Tower refused to be identified by an environment so alien to her nature and expectations. Captivity could not deprive her of the freedom to imagine her tasks and their performance as evidence of an undaunted self—reading, writing, embroidering, and teaching—commit to them, and choose her attitude. She elected to "pick up her jug of misfortune and grief by the tolerable handle" and to see her situation from a positive, even humorous point of view. In the process, she mastered her fate.

We may, similarly, refuse to submit to projected ageism or conventional expectations of behavior patterns of old or elderly people and instead choose to grow to full potential as mature individuals. Like Leonora, we have work to do, and, like her, we need not fear we will run out of projects and therefore try to make each one last as long as possible. She knew they sprang from an inexhaustible source in her own being, which nothing or no one could quell, and we may share that knowledge.

If we analyze Leonora's situation to determine what exactly constitutes challenges—the demonstrated desire for our post retirement lives—we first of all see that we choose those or nothing. Leonora could have turned to the wall and died. The possibility occurred to her as for the first ten days of her incarceration she took no nourishment beyond a little ale and a few slices of lemons. "But my stomach demanded food," she wryly comments. It had overruled her intention to desist a challenge that seemed too burdensome to accept, and her mind, which had wanted to close out the world, once again opened up to its possibilities.

Leonora had repeated one of the most basic processes of life: closing our eyes at night and opening them again to the morning. To most of us this is an insignificant event, miraculous only as we heed it. That discovery is the lynchpin in Beck Weathers' account of his rescue from Everest after being pronounced dead. Exposed to the elements for eighteen hours and in a deep hypothermic coma, he nonetheless opened his eyes, and he saw for the first time the real values in his life, located right in his own backyard. A banal enough realization and scant of evidence for support, as nationwide speaking engagements by now appear to have replaced climbing as a means to feel fully present in the world. All the same, the miracle of opening his eyes induced him to take the first step, and another, and a third till he walked himself into camp and ultimately into rescue engineered by his wife's determined and aggressive operations behind the scenes in faraway California. The Gods help those who help themselves, he might say. To Weathers they extended a miracle.

The opening and closing of our eyes mirror the "constant oscillation between making closures on experiences, then opening up to new experiences" described by Joanne Trautman Banks in her essay on "The Aging Artist: The Sad but Instructive Case of Virginia Woolf." She hypothesizes that Woolf committed suicide due to her ultimate inability to perform the opening and closing of herself to experience. To illustrate her theory, Banks borrows an image from Paul Tillich, the German theologian. Tillich pictures the self as a medieval castle with servants running in and out. That situation is healthy. If, however, a ruler keeps his servants inside, pulls up the drawbridge, stations soldiers on the ramparts, and peers out through the slits in the wall, he will succumb to his own fear and rigidity, suffer a neurosis. If, on the other hand, he leaves his castle without his men and roams so far afield in search of adventure he loses his way back to the castle, he experiences a kind of psychosis. Healthy people move back and forth between the two positions. We arrive at perceptions, draw conclusions and act on those till circumstances make us open our minds to new ideas and we change our minds accordingly.

Leonora did just that. She laid her mind and soul open to the oscillation of opening and closing. She had lost her world and her place in it, been denied the treatment warranted by her rank. Her family were scattered about Europe, and her friends were gone, but she opened her eyes and her mind to the cell, six by seven paces, and herself with "companion" in it, and she found it holding inexhaustible possibilities for pursuit.

She began simply, by setting goals for herself. A physically strong woman, she was given little opportunity to stay fit. Her cell was no park or playing field, but she walked it, back and forth, back and forth. Her skilled, able hands that had reared a family and pulled the strings of court politics she put to work unraveling silk threads from the border of her bed jacket and contrasting strands from her stockings to feed a forgotten needle in the feather down that had pricked her finger on her first night of occupancy in the Tower. A thrown-away rag, four fingers wide, she covered with expert minute stitches, and with a piece of glass she cut double prongs in the wooden handle of a discarded spoon thrown into some rubbish on the floor, for making ribbons. A broken lid from a pewter mug she bent to hold ink made from soot and beer, and with the piece of glass she made a pen from a gnawed off chicken wing. Sugar wrappers turned into notepaper. With a large pin and a piece of chalk she pricked holes in nuts and covered them with chalk to resemble dice for a board game simple enough to be grasped and played by the succession of women who shared her cell. The chalk served for drawing on the table as well and for writing rhymes and hymns.

Nor did she shun political activity. She softened with beer a piece of clay left by the workmen who installed an oven in her cell the first fall she was there and molded it into the shape of a cup which she tricked the castle steward into presenting to the king. The steward was eager to show off the prisoner's handiwork, and King Frederik looked with interest at the piece, especially the bottom on which Leonora had written a petition for clemency. The king and half brother felt sorry for Leonora and expressed an inclination to give the prisoner something with which to while away time, but his Queen, Sophie Amalie, Leonora's rival for power, was unrelenting: Leonora would be permitted nothing.

By the time Sophie Amalie's son ascended the throne, seven years into Leonora's prison term, she had made a life for herself. She had found challenging work. She wrote. Bribing her keepers, she by and by acquired books and paper and started the writing of two memoirs. A book on heroines in history and mythology followed. She volunteered, teaching the successive row of servant women to read, with greater or lesser success, and after the death of her enemy, the dowager queen, accepting the task of ferreting out skeins of silk for the ladies at court and performing elaborate embroidery work. She organized entertainment opportunities. On one occasion she raised her table on end and put a chair on top of it to take turns with her companion to peer out the tiny window down into the castle yard where a tightrope performance was diverting the royal family. On another, she ran upstairs to the top of the Tower to watch a fire, but she ran right back down again to rebuke the castle steward, who in his own excitement to watch the fire had neglected to lock her up.

She squared her spiritual needs as well. God, according to the first of her two memoirs, appears to have been absent from her reflections since the time He saved her and her young siblings from shipwreck on the vessel bringing them to Holland for safekeeping during one of their father's lengthy wars. But He is re-introduced in her second memoir as in her prison life she—somewhat disingenuously—fits herself into the story of Job. Like Job, she posits, who had done nothing but his duty before God and yet suffered successive trials, she had in all her deeds sought to serve her husband and for that had merited the Tower.

Job's story gives her a template for living and offers perspective in her sufferings. It aids her "being loyal to the story" as her twentieth century countrywoman Isak Dinesen advocates. "Accept what life is giving you," Dinesen wrote, "consider it and deal with it. That is the only way to be really alive, which is all that truly matters ... All sorrows can be borne if you put them into a story or tell a story about them." Leonora was made of similar mettle. She could have escaped. For someone who at one time had fled the fortress of Hammershus on the island of Bornholm in the Baltic and who on another occasion had evaded twenty-four guards surrounding her house in Sweden, slipping out of the Blue Tower would have been child's play. One time a piece of wax imprinted with the keys of the prison was smuggled into her cell, and an offer was extended to have the keys made. She thought it a trap and declined the opportunity. Nor were such elaborate measures necessary. She could have picked up the keys lying next to the drunken castle steward and walked out as he took a nap on her servant's bed while Leonora was eating and the servant was gossiping in the hallway.

But her husband was dead and needed her no more; her greater duty was to remain true to herself. Her integrity depended on the king's releasing her as proof of her innocence and the mistake committed by imprisoning her in the first place. After twenty-two years, she obtained her objective. With the monarch's blessing, she was sent to the abandoned Maribo Abbey where she continued the routine she had established in the Tower with only few variations. Ultimately, prison walls had proven no hindrance to someone who had learned to be herself in everything she did—who had learned to love the inexhaustible.

That is perhaps the most important of Leonora's teachings. She did not merely attempt to stay busy or while away the time. She fulfilled her physical, mental, and spiritual needs digging deeply into herself and bringing out the treasures she found and developed as in one motion. She learned to want the inexhaustible, which has its roots in the mind that fashions the task rather than in the task itself. Her story offers few clues as to how we initiate learning that lesson, but the lucky ones among us know that the process is started in childhood.

Inga's brother credits for his initiation the times spent as a child with his grandmother in a summerhouse on the coast of the North Sea. Now and again, he reports, other children would not be available for play or companionship, and he remembers "being bored to death." He wore through that boredom and generated his own company with such success that when the other children showed up, he was almost annoyed at the interruption of the free flow of imagination he was experiencing. A child as fortunate as that has had a peek into the mind's potentially inexhaustible riches and glimpsed at the truth that solitude is a prerequisite for creativity.

If we truly grasp the nature of the inexhaustible, we will also discover that whatever we undertake will lead to the temporary or long-term goals we have set. Leonora's goal was survival, which to her meant demonstrating her integrity. That goal determined her choices: short term ones such as teaching and playing games with her attendants and long term ones such as writing two memoirs, one from birth through the first ten days of her imprisonment, the other styled as a prison diary with a preface to her children arguing the rightness of her decision to remain in prison till she was cleared of suspicion and allegations. A third book, of women in history and mythology—models of heroic behavior—she researched and wrote as her prison terms were gentled by an annual allowance to be spent as she wished and access to an adjoining cell for work and privacy.

If our goal, then, is authenticity, being and becoming the most and best we can be, every choice we make is ruled by that desire and will contribute to its fulfillment. Activities at home and abroad will take on purpose, physical as in walking, hiking, biking, skiing, or rafting; mental as in studies of the Humanities or Sciences; or spiritual as a by-product and reward of absorption in sports, art, music or literature, or in designated "spiritual" activities such as monastic retreats, meditation exercises or studies of sacred texts. Enjoyment follows purpose or becomes itself the purpose as if by a law of nature.

In that mode, we focus our attention, learn as students or disciples do, and avoid the glazed over, discursive looks we bring to exhibits and events or to life itself as idle travelers. When we are really present, we will know the difference between idleness and leisure and spend the latter to acquire purposeful, connective and therefore retainable knowledge, which differs from random information, however diverting, which is bound to be fleeting. Such unconnected information remains a series of "facts" when what we are really likely to want, as Phyllis Rose puts it in her introduction to *The Norton Anthology of Women's Lives*, is "to go beyond the facts of our experience to get to the meaning of it. Which is much harder." And, we may add, much more satisfactory, as it allows us to make associations. The traveler who can see the Iguazu Falls as the Grand Canyon in water and link that vision to the purely horizontal vistas of Glacier Bay and Argentina's Iberian Marshes will have a visual knowledge of the inexhaustible. The Eden-like world of the marshes, where all creatures seek to live in mutual peace, may add to that concept the dimension of time without end.

If we learn by a repeated process of adding new information to old information, new knowledge to old, we will by and by create a larger picture of our worlds and our relation to it. The process may be practiced in any realm of endeavor. When we cook in the spirit of linking new to old, we invite friends and new acquaintances to a dinner party and resist offering only the courses we have served many times before. We explore new culinary territory and new potential friends. The balance between comfort and dare is our conviction that what goes on the chairs is more important than what goes on the table and conversation is the real food of the occasion.

"I always tell people that the best part of the meal for your mind is the conversation," says a Johns Hopkins neurologist. "There is no strong evidence, not much evidence anyway, that anything [e.g. acclaimed "brain foods"] besides basic calories is going to help improve your mind."

We figure, then, that if we have made thoughtful choices for the seats, we can expect stimulating conversation as well as re-affirmation of old and possibilities of new friendships. These are the mental and emotional boons we hope to receive in addition to a well-tickled palate and a pleasingly full stomach.

For an event like that, we imagine a fall setting after everyone has moved indoors and dining rooms once again frame food and conversation. We envision flowers for the table and lots of candles to soften the room and to bring out conversational lumen, the light that travels through space.

Not yet ready to let go of summer's bounty, we will choose her last fruit, brilliant red, yellow and orange peppers, for a starter.

Roasted Peppers as Appetizers

4-5 peppers
¼ cup olive oil
1 ½ T balsamic vinegar
1-2 cloves garlic, peeled and sliced
2 T or so chopped parsley
Salt and pepper
Feta cheese
Baguette

Roast peppers by placing them on a foil-covered baking sheet with top of peppers about 4 inches from broiler element. Turn as pepper skins blacken—process will probably take 20-30 minutes. Put peppers in a paper bag. Close, to steam peppers for about 15 minutes. Peel off blackened skin, remove seeds and slice meat in strips. Serve on slices of baguettes covered with feta cheese. (Peppers may be prepared ahead of time and kept in refrigerator).

Meat of almost any kind makes a good second course, but the mild, rich succulence of lamb is an especially agreeable companion to the pungent flavors of peppers and feta. The following recipe we developed in memory of our culinary explorations on a trip to Greece. We had traveled as a group of enological explorers, so food and wine held high priority, and back in Yakima, we wanted to savor and in some way prolong our adventures. The lamb dish was a main course in our first attempt at a Greek menu, and we were pleased with the outcome.

Boneless, Broiled Leg of Lamb

Leg of lamb, bones and fat removed
2/3-cup olive oil
3 T. lemon juice
1 tsp. salt
½ tsp. black pepper
1 ½ cups onions, thinly sliced
2 T. chopped parsley
2-3 tsp. dried oregano
3 bay leaves, crumbled
3 cloves of garlic, thinly sliced

Cut away any clumps of exposed fat and separate thickest clumps of meat with the point of a knife to make it lie flat. Cut off parchment-like covering. Combine all marinade ingredients. Cover meat with this at least 12 hours, preferably 24, turning meat several times during this period. Wipe off marinade. Broil or grill about 10 to 12 minutes per side. Serve with avgolemono sauce

Avgolemono Sauce

3 egg yolks
1 ½ -2 T. lemon juice
1 tsp. arrowroot (we use cornstarch)
½ tsp. salt
1/8 tsp. Cayenne
1 cup chicken stock
1 T. finely chopped parsley

Over low heat combine in saucepan: egg yolks, lemon juice, cornstarch, salt, and cayenne. Beat together with whisk, then slowly stir in stock. Stir constantly and cook sauce directly over moderate heat until it thickens. When sauce clings to spoon, remove from heat and set over hot, not boiling, water. Stir in parsley just before serving.

This sauce is also great with beef skirt steaks or other red meat, on asparagus or other green vegetables such as broccoli.

Lamb is nicely accompanied by rice, and we have found this *Wild Rice* dish especially suitable.

Wild Rice

1 cup raw wild rice—rinse in strainer
½ pound mushrooms, sliced
1 onion, chopped
½ cup almonds, slivered
¼ cup fresh pepper, chopped
½ cup celery, chopped
¼ cup butter
3 cups chicken broth

Melt butter in Dutch oven; add all other ingredients except chicken broth. Stir until turning yellow. Then add chicken broth. Bake at 325 for 2 hours tightly covered.

A small green salad with a simple dressing of quality olive oil and lemon juice to which we add a spot of Dijon mustard, salt and pepper is a pleasant interlude between main course and dessert.

A menu like this invites a series of wines. The roasted pepper starter is well accompanied by a South Eastern Australian Shiraz, a Lindeman for example, or a Beaujolais Village with a Du Boeuf label, young wines by enough punch to match the peppers. The lamb course deserves a chateaux class wine such as a Chateau Greysac from Medoc: a blend of Cabernet Sauvignon, Merlot, and Cabernet Franc. It is a mellow wine with a pleasant aftertaste. So is St. Michelle's Merlot from Washington State. None of these wines requires extended cellaring and even an all Cabernet Sauvignon from the elegant line of Robert Mondavi labels is enjoyable within five years of production.

For dessert we will move to easy chairs around a coffee table to invite conversation with potentially different tablemates and talk lingering into the night. In that setting, we honor fall with an apple dessert. Any kind will do, apple pies, apple tarts, apple crisps or apple cakes. The *Raw Apple Cake* we feature here is a work in progress especially for Ellie, whose house is surrounded by apple trees providing continuous inspiration. It is very moist and full of orchard flavors.

Raw Apple Cake with Raisins and Walnuts

2 cups flour
2 cups sugar
2 tsp. cinnamon
½ tsp. salt
2 tsp. baking soda
½ cup oil
2 tsp. vanilla
2 eggs
1 cup chopped walnuts
1 cup yellow raisins
4 apples, chopped or grated
(We use steel blade in cuisinart and chop)

Combine flour, sugar, cinnamon, salt and soda and set aside. Beat together the oil, vanilla and eggs. Stir in the walnuts, raisins, and apples. Add dry ingredients all at once and stir until blended. Place batter in a buttered 9-inch tube pan and bake in a 350-degree oven for about 50 minutes, or until a cake tester inserted in center comes out clean. You can use a 9X13 inch pan, in which case you will bake the cake for 40 to 45 minutes. In either case, test for doneness. Frost with *Cream Cheese Frosting*.

Cream Cheese Frosting

¼ cup butter softened
4 ounces cream cheese, softened
1 tsp. vanilla
Pinch of salt
1-1/2 cups sifted powdered sugar (most likely will take 2 cups)

Beat together the cream cheese and butter until mixture is blended. Beat in remaining ingredients until frosting is smooth.

A more challenging dessert, perhaps, would be the French queen of tarts, the *Tarte Tartin* featured in good books on French cooking. It adds a flourish to any evening, especially accompanied with a quality calvados—a suggestion suitable for the *Raw Apple Cake* as well. If, on the other hand, our inspiration does not take us in the direction of apples, a counterpart to the *Tartin* in sophistication and glamour and superb good taste is a chocolate legacy from our English friend Valerie. Val lives on Mill Street leading to Warwick Castle, and her cooking rivals the palatial standards of her environs. In the summer she serves a delectable summer pudding brimming with raspberries and blackberries from surrounding gardens, but on a recent fall visit she delighted us with a *Saint Emilion*, which drew great raves.

Val's Saint Emilion

2/3 cup softened butter
1 ¼ cups confectioners' sugar
1 egg yolk
½ cup warmed milk
4 oz. semi-sweet chocolate
1 T water
½ cup brandy (or as much as it takes)
18 oz. macaroons
One 5 ½ inch Charlotte mold
Frosting:
2 oz semi-sweet chocolate
3 T water
Dab of butter

Cream butter and sugar till soft. Whisk egg yolk and milk together. Melt chocolate and water over saucepan of hot water. When melted, slowly add milk mixture, stirring constantly. Allow to cool. Poor this mixture into butter/sugar. Beat till light and frothy. Grease 5-½ inch Charlotte mold. Mix T water and brandy into a plate. Dip macaroons into this and line bottom and sides of mold (flat sides out). Spoon in a good layer of the chocolate cream; cover with a layer of macaroons and rest of chocolate cream. Finish with a layer of macaroons. Cover it with a plate that fits the mold and place a weight on it. Leave in refrigerator overnight. Turn out on a serving plate. Make chocolate icing by melting water, butter and chocolate. Pour over cake. Enjoy.

A snifter of cognac or armagnac adds to the glamour and makes the accompanying coffee taste even better.

An evening like this leaves guests and hosts equally satisfied and in ready agreement that life at any stage may be good indeed.

5

HOW DO WE KNOW WE ARE
LIVING THE GOOD LIFE?

As you set out for Ithaka
Hope your road is a long one,
Full of adventure, full of discovery...
To learn and go on learning from those who know.

Keep Ithaka always in your mind.
Arriving there is what you're destined for.
But don't hurry the journey at all.
Better it lasts for years,
So you are old by the time you reach the island, ...
Wise as you have become, so full of experience,
You'll have understood by then what these Ithakas
Mean.

— Constantine Cavafy

S uppose we didn't know how old we are. How old would we
then think ourselves to be? Given no indicators, such as birth
records or photographs taken in the course of a life time, we might
answer according to how we feel on a given day, younger when our
bodies are working well, the sun is shining and people around us
are pleasant and helpful, older when we wake up on a gray morning
with creaking joints. Such an answer would suggest that biological,
not chronological age is what matters. Yet, we know that neither is

really what writes the text for any age because age, as much as gender, is a social construct dictating social behaviors.

We start school at five or six, are expected to be independently working and providing for ourselves after graduating from college, or even high school, and likely to retire at about the age of sixty-five—regardless of biological or chronological readiness for any of those three stages.

Not only does such acculturation prescribe behaviors and expectations for each phase; it ascribes value to each and generally labels the middle period "best," the flowering of our potential for power and acquisition, the fulfillment of our Puritan heritage with its dictates of hard work and promise of rewards. Those are the years we can really show our stuff, make a mark on the world. Our buying into that assessment offers a reason for the gap between ability on the part of "Third Stagers" and the opportunities offered us for demonstration, the plangent lament of professional women we have cited. We have no reason to believe that mental acuity, knowledge and skills acquired in the course of careers spanning some forty years have been lost with our entering retirement. Yet the social barriers of stereotyping hindering their full employment may corrode our confidence and stall our enterprise. Additionally, the disconnect between what we can do and opportunities for doing may make us question the standards by which our culture assesses our life span. Were we to propose that our lives in retirement are potentially as rich and fulfilling as our lives in the market place, what evidence could we bring to bear and what would be the standards testing the proposition that "the good life" does not come to an end at the cessation of "getting and spending"?

Back in the sixties, Marya Mannes, writer and daughter of musicians, asked herself and her readers the question of how we might determine the quality of a painting, play or composition if we did not have critics to tell us. "By what standards," she wrote, "by what values would we decide whether they [unsigned paintings at an exhibit] were good or bad, talented or untalented, successes or failures? How can we ever know what we think is good?"

The question she posed addresses the synchronicity between external instruction, the words of critics eliciting our acceptance or rejection of a work of art, and internalized education, which, ideally, will result in individual refinement of powers of discrimination, the ability to tell good from bad, value from dross. Mannes proceeded to decry her contemporaries' tendency to deny the validity of criteria and standards acquired through experience and education and subsequently imposed on a given piece of art. The denial of critical standards is a popular approach, she observed, because it relieves the critic of the "responsibility of judgment" and the public of the "necessity of knowledge." As a one-time president of CBS television opined at a hearing before the Federal Communication Commission, "One man's mediocrity is another man's good program," his way of acknowledging that personal taste is the determiner, and no values are absolute.

The danger inherent in such ready acceptance of whatever leaps the transom of our consciousness is evident in current popular culture, which embraces the "trend," values the newness of things and ideas, celebrates the young, and chucks the old as probably not worthwhile. Grand advances in science and technology support the theory that "new" is best, and our extended lives give it proof. Yet, the speed, the comfort, the productivity and duration of our life's journey do not define or measure the reason we travel. Nor do they answer the question of why we are here and whether we lead the good life, which is always *more* than speed, duration, comfort and productivity.

That *something more* which constitutes the good life we are given occasion and opportunity to explore in the Third Stage. We may seek to divine its nature; and we may apply critical criteria and standards acquired by education and experience to evaluate its quality. As arbiters and critics of our own lives, we can make an effort to challenge, perhaps transcend or transform the values accorded the stages of our lives by the society we inhabit.

Evaluation of ourselves and our place in the world we consider important because we ultimately realize that personal fulfillment, ourselves as work in progress, may be fully achieved only as society at large begins to groove with the needs and capabilities of the Third Stage population and when that group perceives and is itself perceived as a cultural vanguard.

It is unrealistic to imagine ourselves as "wise elders" in a technological society. It is, however, within the realm of probability for our group to lead lives looking forward with educated and expectant minds and contemplative attitudes rather than backwards with nostalgic longings for a vision of a world we cannot duplicate.

May Sarton celebrated her seventieth birthday in that spirit. "I do not feel old at all," she wrote, "not as much a survivor as a person still on her way. I suppose real old age begins when one looks backward rather than forward, but I look forward with joy to the years ahead and especially to the surprises that any day may bring."

With Sarton for a role model and social critics like Marya Mannes for mentors, we may share in their insights and profit from their "templates." As a means to forge standards for evaluation, for example, Mannes writes, "it is fairly obvious that the more you read and see and hear, the more equipped you'll be to practice that art of association which is at the basis of all understanding and judgment. The more you live and the more you look, the more aware you are of a consistent pattern—as universal as the stars, as the tides, as breathing, as night and day—underlying everything. I would call this pattern and this rhythm an order. Not order—an order. Within it exists an incredible diversity of forms. Without it lies chaos. I would further call this order—this incredible diversity held within one pattern—health. And I would call chaos—the wild cells of destruction—sickness. It is in the end up to you to distinguish between the diversity that is health and the chaos that is sickness, and you can't do this without a process of association that can link a bar of Mozart with the corner of a Vermeer painting, or a Stravinsky score with a Picasso abstraction; or that can relate an aggressive act with a Franz Kine painting and a fit of coughing with a John Cage composition."

A daughter of artists and herself a writer, Mannes may be raising the bar too high for most of us to attempt the jump, but though we may not be able to make those artistic leaps, we can at least refrain from subscribing to every new slogan that comes down the pike and see in it a recipe for living. As Morris Berman asserts in *The Twilight of American Culture*, "thinking" does not have to mean "nothing more than wandering through the latest theme park of slogans," which inevitably results in "the inability of the American public to distinguish garbage from quality; in fact ... [they] identify garbage *as* quality." Hence the success of the New Age industry, which relies on the premise that our rational minds are our worst enemy.

Professional women who are trained to think in our disciplines do not in retirement have to discard everything we know as so much baggage. We do not have to agree that everything we will ever need to know we learned in kindergarten or read books with titles like *Escaping the Prison of the Intellect.* We can choose instead to participate in "the great conversation" Mortimer Adler envisioned as associate editor of the *Great Books of the Western World.* Readers, he imagined, would internalize the author's ideas, reflect upon them and arrive at insights of their own. He shared with Mannes the insight into knowledge and intelligence that our thoughts, feelings, and actions are part of the order underlying the diversity of the world. It is our task, therefore, to connect passionate pursuit in whatever field or realm to the bedrock of our intrinsic selves. Our brains are wired to draw on and assimilate knowledge from a variety of sources. We have only to make the effort and continue to make it.

For models of women making that effort, we may explore the fictional sub-genre called the *Reifungsroman,* a German word like the better-known *Bildungsroman* which depicts the growing up process of a young man or woman. A *Reifungsroman* focuses on characters "ripening" into middle and old age. Most are written by women and about women, perhaps because mature women outnumber mature men as a market, but more likely due to the fact that women have been confronted more brutally than men with the specter of ageism in a sexist and youth-oriented culture. Likely, that confrontation, actively felt or passively observed, may have led the way to anger, fuelling articulation on the part of these women writers. With their interpretations of "the social and psychological experience of aging by the female body and mind, [they] move beyond patriarchal paradigms of human development ... " and thereby "perform an invaluable service," wrote Barbara Frey Waxman in *From the Hearth to the Open Road*.

The books she chose for illustration of "women's rite of passage into senescence" show aging women's commitments and interests, their "physical and psychological pain; loneliness, alienation from family and youthful society; self doubt; feeling of uselessness, and grief over the loss of friends, mental acuity, and physical energy." But they also celebrate the "opening up of life for many of these aging heroines as they literally [or metaphorically] take to the open road in search of themselves and new roles in life." They show these women developing and expanding more "as they grow old than they did as they grew up—or perhaps they truly grow up at last ... If the protagonist of a *Reifungsroman* dies at the end of the story, it is commonly after she has grown in a significant way." The intimacy of these narratives, sometimes conceived as journals, allows readers of any age to identify with the lives of aging women, experience their hopes and longings as well as their frustrations. They invite perception of them as real human beings; a feat too rarely accomplished by gerontology and psychology texts.

Collectively, such *Reifungsromane*, Waxman points out, engender identification with potentially "psychological and social consequences. Younger readers may acknowledge elders as part of the human community while also acquiring greater understanding of and preparation for their own passage into middle age and senescence. Older readers may gain a fuller perspective on what they are experiencing, as well as reaffirmation of their humanity. Both attitudinal changes challenge the ageism that young and old often feel."

As a means of resistance to ageism and a challenge to the authority of youth, such texts may ultimately foster "a will for change" in a society which has failed to realize that unlike sexism, racism, and classism, which will affect only some, old age will ultimately claim for its victims all its members *fortunate enough* to live that long. As a force for change then, such novels may help all of us to interact more sensitively with neighbors, coworkers and friends as they and we all "ripen" and help us remember with May

Sarton that "it is possible to keep the genius of youth into old age, the curiosity, the intense interest in everything from a bird, to a book, to a dog."

For readers who would like a more specific approach to combating despair and fragmentation—our frequent companions during later years—Sarton's heroine Caro Spencer in Waxman's interpretation of *As We Are Now* offers a program outlining five ways: "through keeping a journal; through maintaining and refueling her anger at her unjust treatment; through reminiscing about relationships from her past; through reaching out to the other residents [of the nursing home], the local clergyman, her daughter, and [a friend]; and ... through planning, without fear, her own death."

Choosing middle-aged and old women for protagonists, the writers of these *Reifungsromane* make readers acknowledge the protagonists' undiminished womanliness with its yearning for intimacy and touch. They envision them as inhabitants of a continuum, each life cycle feeding into the next, as all of us must come to experience it in order to transition ourselves out of an ageist society towards a utopia of agelessness.

Books like those, represented by works of May Sarton, Marya Mannes, Alice Adams, Barbara Pym, and Doris Lessing, to mention just a handful, assist our graduation from stereotypes and prejudice and suggest other standards by which to interpret and measure the quality of our lives and the lives of others. To acquire those, we may act upon Mannes's suggestion that reading, seeing and hearing are the foundation of pattern recognition, which she claims to be the basis for understanding and judgment. That basis all of us can furnish. We can learn to discern the patterns in our own lives, in the lives of others and in the ways in which they intersect, a discernment which enables us to write the life stories that tell us who we are and who we may become.

As the *Reifungsromane* show, each story is different and yet tangential to the others, and it is for each of us to write our own text in living it and in that way bring into life the collective tale of professional women in the Third Stage of our lives. Mannes uses pieces of art as examples of associations, but the process of association is equally valid as applied to our lives and everything we do. The traveler abroad who can link the music she hears, the pictures she sees, the buildings she visits, the food she buys and cooks or merely eats to one another and herself will enrich her experience above that of a tourist who sees each for what it is but not for what it represents.

The writers of memoirs will perforce make associations between past and present happenings and in the process perceive a pattern, which will guide future events and decisions. The practiced reader will forge links among images, plots and characters of different authors and not only remember all of those more clearly due to recall of associations but will see patterns as options for structuring her own life. Travelers, writers and readers will see themselves in multiple ways, and in the tapestry woven by application of education and experience they may catch a glimpse of the "figure in the carpet"—their true selves.

This figure may at first be dimly and only temporarily perceived, but attention and work will bring it out, and knowledge and experience will form a triad with instinct to adjudicate its worth. Our attitude, the freedom to choose how we perceive ourselves and our circumstances, will determine to what extent we want to refashion the picture. We are the arbiters—not random events or happenstance imposed by outside forces or our aging bodies, which must by and large be contained—but we ourselves are in charge of our life stories and—within reason—we can change what we decide needs changing.

Travel, reading, and writing diaries or memoirs help us discern the figure in the carpet, as may any other pursuit we lend time and attention. Each of Jeannette's quilts says something about who she is. Its purpose—a gift, display or sale—says something about her own purpose and commitment. She may or may not be consciously aware of that, but her enjoyment in their making would let her know the work she does is in tune with her being.

Similarly, Joan's garden tells us, and possibly her as well, volumes about who she is if only we can read the text. The book of recipes the mother gave her son as a graduation present suggests a pattern of their lives together, as family photos on a wall or in a scrapbook speak their silent language of family history and family patterns revealing the "struggle of memory against forgetting," the insistence of soul on knowing who we are.

When we can see our lives as a contiguous whole, as a pattern, we can know it is good, and if it is not, we may see how to change it. As Isak Dinesen opined, we can endure anything in life if only we can write it into a story. That, she said, would allow us to see a design in our actions no matter how unrelated they may appear, as a story writer imposes order on her material and lets us see the large picture which remains obscure in the working out of details.

To illustrate her point, Dinesen relates in *Out of Africa* a story she heard as a child, "The Road of Life." The narrator, she wrote, would illustrate the tale as he told it. In a house with a round window, a triangular garden, and a pond nearby lived a man, who one night woke up to hear a terrible noise. He took the road to the pond, running to the south where he stumbled over a big stone in the middle of the road. A bit later he fell into a ditch, got up, fell into another, got up, fell into a third and again got up. Then he realized he had taken the wrong road and headed north.

Again the noise seemed to be coming from the south and he ran back, repeating the stumble and fell. He now could hear that the noise came from one end of the pond, so he rushed there and saw that water was gushing out. He stopped the leakage and went back to bed. The next morning as he looked out his window, he saw that his motions in the night had traced the picture of a stork.

"I will remember that story," she writes "in the hour of need. The man in the story was cruelly deceived, and had obstacles put in his way. He must have thought, 'What ups and downs. What a run of bad luck!' He must have wondered what was the idea of all his trials, he could not know that it was a stork. But through them all he kept his purpose in view, nothing made him turn round and go home, he finished his course, he kept his faith. That man had his reward. In the morning he saw the stork. He must have laughed out loud then. The tight place, the dark pit in which I am now lying, of what bird is it the talon? When the design of my life is completed, shall I, shall other people see a stork?" Or something else, perhaps?

Perceived shapes or forms, as A.S. Byatt points out, are not closures, only guidance.

All the same, Dinesen reminds us, our determination to fashion a purpose and seek to fulfill it will reward us with containment of the seemingly irrelevant ups and downs. In addition, our lives will be seen by others for what they are, tempered by the observer's powers of observation and standards of discrimination, as the stork, Juno's bird, to one interpreter suggests filial piety and to another, traveler in the world. That is the risk a writer takes as he proffers his book and the risk all of us take as we live our lives, write our stories. We all furnish "biographies" for one another.

"We are communal histories, communal books," as Michael Ondaatje observed in *The English Patient*. All we can hope for are discriminating readers. In turn, we can practice being those ourselves.

Dinesen's story furthermore points out that as in our Third Stage we take ourselves on as works in progress and seek connections between our developing selves and our actions, we must guard against taking too narrow a view of what is "relevant" to our development of self. To the man in the story, all the ups and downs must have seemed irrelevant to his effort at stopping the leakage, but he remained unperturbed, kept up his search and learned that all his vicissitudes were part of his life's pattern. Relevance is a tricky concept and those of us who have spent our lives in education have heard the clamor from students demanding only courses and texts, which they perceive as "relevant." It is reasonable to want a voice in the discussion of one's education, but when we are young we rarely know what will and will not take on significance for our lives and futures. If our sense of self and its potential is too narrow, and we see information as useful only as it relates directly to our current situation, we run the danger of straitjacketing ourselves mentally, confining ourselves to thinking in a box. If unthinkingly we spurn, for example, what due to lack of knowledge at the time may seem random lectures and travels and measure our patience for listening to someone else's reminiscences to the degree to which they are directly applicable to our immediate lives, we may severely shortchange ourselves.

Who knows what chance phrase or evocative sound may call up those deeper layers in us, which will uncover the figure in the carpet? The only safeguard against mental and spiritual constriction is our forging a clear enough and large enough perception of who we are that we may learn what is and what is not relevant, what is and what is not "good" in Mannes's sense of the word.

So let us pose that we assume responsibility for ourselves in accordance with individual inclination and energy and make considerate and discriminatory choices for living our lives. In doing so, we inhabit the world, the society which we call home, and we realize that our actions have an effect there for which we must assume responsibility as well. Ironically, we live at a time to experience a rise of consumer culture even as we realize that we can no longer buy in order to be. That complicates the issue.

Third Stagers are increasingly perceived as targets of the commercial world with advertisers seeking to profit from our collective buying power even as we ourselves know that we need fewer and fewer things. This high profiling of our population may be used to advantage, however, if we can see a way to make ourselves visible, not by our purchasing power and material indulgences, but by living and advocating the values education and experience have taught us to cherish. That is an elitist attitude based on a belief that without a hierarchy of values, an order, as Mannes put it, civilization cannot exist; but elitism does not necessarily preclude validity.

Thoughtful men and woman of our time, among them Morris Berman, have pointed to the decline of American civilization in terms of increasing social and economic inequality; increasing loss of entitlements (notably social security and Medicare); rapidly dropping levels of literacy, critical understanding, and general intellectual awareness; "spiritual death—emptying out of cultural content and the freezing (or repackaging) of it in formu- las—kitsch."

Alarm and regret characterize their pronouncements and challenge us to consider whether such allegations demand our response. Aren't we vestiges of the dwindling middle class? Recipients of social security checks and Medicare? A literate, skeptical, intellectually aware "cohort"? Vibrant, thinking human beings? And, as importantly, aren't we cut out of the world in which "goods" means the good life because we no longer need lots of things and buying no longer equals being? Where does that put us in terms of moral responsibility but in a place of authentic thought and its corollary, authentic living?

We might begin by deciding for ourselves that it is healthy to rebel against forces and social norms that define, categorize and classify us, specifically in terms of youth and beauty. Statistics show that cosmetic surgery is on the increase—for both men and women—regardless of potential short or long-term harm caused by such procedures. We may decline the invitation to sign up and with our disavowal, as Frida Kerner Furman argues, signal a feminist response at two levels: "At a personal level, it refuses the potential loss for women of embodied personal integrity. At a collective level, it has the potential to serve as a collective strategy by speaking to the power of women as consumers to influence market conditions."

An example of such resistance to social trends deemed unacceptable is the video *West Coast Crones,* which features a group of older women in San Francisco who meet to examine, evaluate and, if necessary, debunk dominant cultural expectations for women and decline wearing the labels our culture places on us as old, ugly, and worthless. They refuse to be seen from the vantage point of others, which frequently means they remain invisible. They demand visibility. They insist on looking back, staring down the specter of ageism, no matter how potent. Precisely such a stare meets us in a recently issued stamp featuring Edna Ferber, a writer of the 1924 bestseller *So Big.* Steely eyes in a visage only slightly less gray than her hat, dress and pearls dominate the face of the 83 cent stamp used for mailings overseas as the post office runs out of 80 cent denominations. A left-handed gesture to a Pulitzer Prize winner.

Resistance comes at a price, but we can all "let our lives speak," as the Quaker saying has it, and in so doing attempt to invert the factors of bipolarization, young versus old, rich versus poor, black versus white, men versus women. Beerman's *Twilight of American Culture* points the way toward a vision of a social contract obligating all of us to uphold the values undergirding the good life as we envision it. "If social inequality is on the rise ... then the attempt to close the gap between rich and poor—the socialist tradition—is one of our greatest treasures. If corporate values are turning our citizens into mindless consumers, then the healthy 'elitist' intellectual tradition of our civilization—history, philosophy, literature—is another treasure we have to fight for, and hand down. If the masses zone out on *Titanic* and *Wayne's World* at the Cineplex, there is the whole world of Truffaut and Kurosawa, which could conceivably inspire a new generation of filmmakers and moviegoers. For every ... dean who ... makes no distinction between higher education and marketing, there are a few faculty members willing to stand up to her and tell her that there is no substitute for direct personal involvement and painstaking intellectual apprenticeship." Berman concludes his book by saying, "I believe ... that the rewards of a life lived in terms of quality, as opposed to kitsch, are enormous," and, we will add, such a life reverberates beyond the sphere of the individual.

Berman's is not a lone cry. Beginning in the mid nineties, voices have been raised around the land and abroad crying out the need for a collective story to provide a pattern for life in the Age of Technology and specifically for life in the Third Stage. "The Technology God enslaves and gives no profound answers in the bargain," warns a contemporary Canadian writer. "We are left at last with no loom to weave a fabric to our lives ... we need a story that will help us to be people with an elementary sense of justice, the ability to see things as others do, a sense of transcendental responsibility, optimal wisdom, good taste, courage, compassion and faith."

That story senior citizens have to tell "anyone who is prepared to listen," assert Sandra Cusack and Wendy Thomsen in their rallying text *Leadership for Older Adults*, based on the premise that everyone needs to contribute and society needs everyone's contribution. For illustration they showcase two senior centers, one with shared, one with authoritarian leadership, each reflecting "common leadership issues in retirement organizations throughout the Western world." Over time, they argue, feminism has found a voice and multiculturalism has become a political agenda. It is now time, "to conquer the last deadly 'ism.' Ageism is insidious, subtle and pervasive, affecting not just senior citizens but all members of society. We must recognize and eradicate it. No society can be healthy that fails to honor and respect its senior citizens, and *no individual can be healthy who shrinks from the image of a future self.*" [Emphasis added]

Cusack and Thompson appear to define the "we" who must do something as society in general and senior citizens in particular, which then raises the issue of whether we could, should, or would count ourselves among them and if so, on what grounds, by what standards? A look at Paul Fussell's witty, satirical and irreverent book *Class* offers a clue to the identity of individuals he and Morris Berman envision as standard bearers of values. *Class* debunks the American myth of equality and divides society into nine classes from "top out-of-sight" to "bottom out-of-sight" with upper, middle and low in between, each defined by money, appearance and speech.

Most interesting in this context is the "category" that has dealt itself out of all these classes. He labels them "X persons," *not to be confused with Generation X as we know it.* They are people who have earned X-personhood by a strenuous effort of discovery "in which curiosity and originality are indispensable ... They tend to be self-employed, doing what social scientists call autonomous work ... and freedom from supervision is one of [their] most obvious characteristics. X people are independent-minded, free of anxious regard for popular shibboleths ... They adore the work they do, and they do it until they are finally carried out, 'retirement' being a concept meaningful only to hired personnel or wage slaves who despise their work ... X category is a sort of unmonied aristocracy."

Fussell's characteristics of X-persons defy ageism, sexism and racism in their invitation to anyone who is curious and willing to be original. No barriers or stereotypes prevent admittance. Even the label of being "unpatriotic" cannot be affixed the X-ers, he claims, "people fearful that X-hood may be somehow un-American should realize that, on the contrary, it is firmly in the American grain. Knowing that, Mark Twain created an exemplary category-X person and said when first introducing him, 'Huckleberry came and went, at his own free will.'" Fussell's *Class* was written twenty years ago, but his call to action in a voice half serious, half tongue in cheek, echoes in a Letter to the Editor in *The Yakima Herald Tribune* on August 17, 2004. In his exhortation to "join the $25 army," Brett Dillahunt writes:

> While we like to think that democratic principles still hold sway in Washington D.C. and Olympia I'm afraid the truth is that our nation is no longer governed, it's owned. The money to finance [presidential] campaigns comes from every big business and wealthy individual you can think of, but a few of us Washingtonians would like to try something different.
>
> We are meeting in Seattle, Yakima, Spokane and other cities, in small groups, and pledging $25 apiece to our favorite candidate, along with a Top 10 list of issues each group would like them to address. These checks and lists are then collected and delivered straight to the campaign offices of the candidates each group chooses.
>
> If only one voter in six participates in this movement, we can replace all special interest donors in every campaign in America. Think of it—$25 once every two years—that's just over a dollar a month ... We are nonpartisan and all volunteer. We have no revenue, no bank accounts and no lawyers, just a Web site and plenty of good will, as we would much rather have your participation instead of your money.

Fussell just might applaud that Washingtonian's take on his idea of X-hood.

Sharing Fussell's intent but speaking in quite a different voice is David Maitland's *Aging As Counterculture: A Vocation for the Later Years*, which argues that the elderly constitute a counterculture in their detachment from dominant cultural attitudes. That affords them, he observes, an objective vantage point from which to evaluate and potentially challenge existing socio-cultural values along the line of re-constructing old age.

Freedom to be who we are at any age with a will to elide or combat obstacles forged by stereotyping age groups is a right worth our insistence. Soon enough we shall have critical mass in a population that in the U.S. will double its sixty-five-year-olds by the year 2030. It is none too soon to envision, as Morris Berman does, a dawn succeeding the twilight. "I imagine," he writes, "once again, a vibrant middle class, strong continuity with enlightenment traditions of democracy and expanding intellectual inquiry, and a culture in which the arts, sciences, and literature play a central role in the lives of a very large percentage of the population. I also imagine a civilization with strong humanistic values, in which business and cyber technology play an ancillary role. The world of commerce and video display terminals would be, in the New Enlightenment, regarded as a tool of the good life, but no one would make the mistake of confusing it with the good life. Accordingly, corporations would exist on a much smaller scale than they do now, and their influence would be correspondingly diminished. Indeed, it couldn't be otherwise, because after the Great Collapse of the late twenty-first century, it would become clear to everybody that corporate control of our lives was a toxic arrangement, finally responsible for the crash, and that now, during the period of reconstruction, it must be avoided at all costs. Along with this, then, there would be a healthier balance between global and regional culture. For one thing, MacWorld, and the Coca-colonization of the planet, would be things of the past."

Berman's utopian fantasy may be over the top for practical thinkers' and doers' view of the world from the trenches, but it nonetheless resonates in even such popular texts as Marc Freedman's *How Baby Boomers Will Revolutionize Retirement and Transform America*. Marc Freeman sees Third Stage men and women returning to education, contributing to society, and working on their own projects. Characterizing them as "adaptable, flexible, mobile, experienced and global professionals," he imagines Third Stagers seeking outlets for their talents and skills in Experience Corps, Centers of Un-Retirement, Senior Peace Corps or as "Parachuting Retirees" coming in to do short-term projects like consulting, administrating, or teaching.

We will add to Freeman's an *alternate* vision of retired individuals as a group of people who choose to spend time thinking and reflecting and in doing so responding to a call that rivals that for productivity. For that contingent, Norman Cousins may be tapped as a spokesman. "We in America have everything we need except the most important thing of all—time to think, and the habit of thought," he observed. "Thought is the basic energy in human history. Civilization is put together not by machines but by thought. Leadership today requires not so much a determination to outsmart the other fellow as an understanding of the lessons of human experience."

For the drought of thought, we are all responsible, he alleges. "There is no point in passing the buck or looking for guilty parties. We got where we are because of the busy man in the mirror."

Cousins' concern about "the busy man in the mirror" is further emphasized by Richard Restak, professor of neurology at George Washington University Medical Center. He alleges as a source for the "explosive increase in attention deficit disorder—ADD—the emphasis on a staccato style of verbal communication—that is, the sound bite. As television critics have been pointing out for decades, television does not lend itself to fine-grained analysis of serious issues. That's because television is an emotionally engaging pictorial medium that primarily addresses the right hemisphere of the brain, whereas thought and logic involve entirely different parts of the brain, predominantly the left hemisphere. As a result of this shift from words to pictures, from thoughtful reflection to emotional involvement, many of us experience difficulty when called upon to evaluate complex issues that require reasoned analysis rather than sound-bite-level responses. We concentrate less on issues and policies than on whether we can 'identify with' a candidate, whether he 'seems believable,' and whether we conclude he 'comes across' well on television."

Restak furthermore argues that the shift from left to right hemisphere processing has resulted in our increasingly shorter attention span and greater difficulty in being really present for one another. He cites the example of a couple having lunch after meeting at a party and wanting to get to know one another better.

They are engaged in conversation. As he talks, he looks over her right shoulder at a television showing a game in progress, and she interrupts their interlude with ten minutes on her cell phone. Neither gives full attention to the other. Both sacrifice real talk, the personal encounter demanding attention and presence, in favor of a "technology-mediated interaction," as background television images tend to capture our attention even if we try to ignore it and cellular phones split our presence between our immediate and virtual reality.

To clinch his argument, Restak quotes Sven Birkets, a literary critic, who sees all of us immersed in "the great mediation ... We have put between ourselves and the natural world so many layers of signals, noises, devices and habits that the chance for ... connection is very limited."

We have sought instances of such "connection" with our suggestions of fuller engagement in family and friends, shared readings and writings, group participation in arts and sports events, as well as our series of dinners celebrating the passing seasons with conversation and companionship. Finally, at year's end when Christmas and New Year's give occasions for parties, we extend a virtual invitation to a festivity not centered on the dinner table, but giving incitement by a performance to bring about the group synergy, which is the hallmark of any gathering.

In past centuries, drawing rooms and salons served as venues for friends and acquaintances, who would gather to enjoy an artistic performance and the inspiration it provided for constructive social intercourse and conviviality. Such events might showcase a musical or dramatic entertainment, sometimes by a famous artist, such as Chopin in Paris and Schubert in Vienna, or simply by guests with special talents. The movie *Breaker Morant* features such a scene, as do the films built on Jane Austen's novels. In this country, the Kennedy White House broadcast extravagant salon occasions. But much less will do, and in our experience, holiday time has proven a festive and fertile time for "salons."

Drawing rooms or, if those are neither available nor large enough, "party rooms" in condominiums or shared housing provide intimate settings for musical and literary performance. We were fortunate to have for a while at Central Washington University a retired opera singer. He taught in the music department there and graciously accepted an invitation to bring some of his students for a performance in Inga's drawing room. A soprano, an alto, a tenor and a bass arrived, who had been practicing for a performance of *Tosca*. They sang their arias and duets as their teacher accompanied them on the piano and told the "story" linking the musical pieces.

Equally suitable for drawing rooms are Liederabends featuring songs which are best enjoyed in intimate settings with decent acoustics. We count among our friends a young pianist who grew up in Yakima and who married a California soprano while studying in Vienna. Back in Yakima on Christmas or summer vacations, they can be persuaded to give a recital of songs interspersed with piano solos, as was the custom of the *Schubertiades*, evenings featuring Schubert's Lieder. Schubert and his friends would gather at someone's residence to sing his songs interspersed with pieces for the piano.

Schubertiades have experienced a recent revival world-wide and now include well-advertised concerts on a rather larger scale, such as the New York City gathering, the "Alternative Schubertiade," called by Phil Kline to "devise music whose departure point was, in one way or another Schubertian," or drawing room performances like one described in the *Santa Monica Mirror*, performed in the home of Dr. Robert Winter and featuring a pianist, a violinist, and a soprano.

For us, yet another avenue to artistic performance has been our Thursday Reader group whose members boast talented children in music or drama. They have come home from college for Christmas vacation and enjoyed performing before friends of their parents. On one occasion, an aspiring opera singer brought excerpts of her recent recital and divided the program between it and Christmas songs, ending the evening with everyone singing "Oh Come All Ye Faithful" as the white candles on the Christmas tree burnt to their sockets.

We also know of a hostess who invited a student to do a one-woman recital of Wallace Shawn's *The Fever*, which she had prepared for her Master's degree in drama. Sharon was pleased to have an opportunity to present her show to an intimate group especially because the play is intended for drawing room performance. It was a great success. For two hours, interrupted by a short intermission and glasses of wine, the audience paid rapt attention in the close proximity of performer and listeners.

Our examples show that even in a small town, possibilities abound for any hostess who will take the trouble to look about for talented people, young and old, who might welcome the opportunity to stage a drawing room performance. In metropolitan areas, odds are even better. Artists, in general, like to perform. We can let it be our task to provide the stage.

Wine and hors d'oeuvres make enjoyable follow-ups, and we offer some suggestions, though of course the field is wide open. Anything is tasty as conversation flows from stimulated minds celebrating the winter solstice with its promise of returning light to our hemisphere and to our lives.

Tex Mex

1st layer: refried beans
2nd layer: avocados (mashed) or guacamole
3rd layer: 2 T lemon juice
4th layer: ½ t. salt and ¼ t. pepper
5th layer: a mixture of 1 cup sour cream, ½ cup mayo, and 1 pkg. Taco Season mix
6th layer: 1 can of chopped chilies
7th layer: bunch of chopped chilies
8th layer: 2 chopped tomatoes
9th layer: black olives, chopped
10th layer: 8 ounces shredded cheese

Shrimp Salad Spread

2 three oz. pkgs. cream cheese
1 ½ T blue cheese
1 ½ cups mayonnaise

1 T horseradish
1 medium sour pickle, chopped
1 clove garlic, minced
3 pounds shrimp, cooked, peeled and chopped
¼ cup minced scallions
½ small white onion, grated
1 t. chopped pimento
6 dashes Tabasco
½ t. salt
1 T paprika

Cream cheese and mayonnaise. Add rest of ingredients. Serve with rye rounds.

Goat Cheese Spread

8 oz. goat cheese
4 oz. cream cheese
1 t. minced garlic
½ cup chopped chives
1 t. paprika

Mix all ingredients well and add a little milk to thin the spread and make it smoother. Serve on crackers or slices of baguette.

Cheese Covered Grapes

1 pound seedless large grapes (about 50)
10 oz. pecans
4 T crumbled Roquefort cheese
1 8 oz. pkg. cream cheese
2 T heavy cream

Wash grapes and pat dry. Crush pecans on a platter or sheet of waxed paper. Combine Roquefort, cream cheese, and cream them in a bowl, mixing well. Roll grapes in cheese mixture and then in pecans, coating well. Chill, covered, till serving.

Salmon Pate

7 oz. cooked salmon (or halibut)
8 oz. cream cheese
1 T lemon juice
1 T grated onion
1 t. horseradish
¼ t. liquid smoke
½ cup chopped walnuts or pecans
3 T chopped parsley

Combine salmon, cream cheese, lemon juice, onion, horseradish, and liquid smoke in food processor or blender. Process till smooth. Stir in chopped nuts and parsley and transfer to a crock. Refrigerate until ready to serve. Serve with crackers, baguette slices or Swedish knackerbrod.

Val's Best Gravlax

One fillet of salmon, about 1 ½ pounds, skin on
2 ½ oz. coarse salt
3 ½ oz. sugar
1 T white peppercorns, crushed
Bunch of fresh dill—chopped
1 t. brandy

Rub combined salt, sugar and peppercorns onto fillet. Cover with the dill, sprinkle with brandy. Cut fillet in half and place one piece on top of the other, skins to the outside. Put the "packet" of salmon into a plastic bag, place it in a dish and put a weight on top. Store in refrigerator. Turn 3-4 times a day for 3 days. Baste daily with accumulated liquid.

Mustard Dill Sauce

Mix in a non-aluminum bowl
3 T sugar

1 ½ t. dry mustard
3 T distilled white vinegar
1 T marinade from gravlax
6 T mild prepared mustard

Whisk in approximately 6 oz light sunflower or vegetable oil. Add 2-3 t. chopped dill leaves. Refrigerate for at least 1 hour. Serve with gravlax.

Wines to accompany such an occasion may be furnished by the host and hostess, who may then choose to serve jug wines like the ones we described in Chapter Three. Or guests might be asked to contribute to a wine tasting of red or white varietals, such as Merlots or Syrahs among the reds and Chardonnays, Fume Blancs, dry wines, or the sweeter Rieslings among the whites.

We cannot know whether any attempt at authentic life has any importance in the history we are writing as we live it, but we can know that with no attempt to maintain what we think is worth valuing in our lives and culture, we can go no way but down. Someone has to hold up the day, provide a vision. Why not us? We are individuals with no agenda other than to live the good life in Emerson's terms, with self-respect emanating from self-reliance. How can we know such lives are ineffective when we know for a fact that the immediate personal benefit of preservation of values is huge?

How can we think otherwise as we stand reminded by Norman Cousins' insistence that "progress proceeds out of elusive but vital fractions. Sudden spurts in the condition of a society come about as the result of small achievements with high symbolic content. The probability of such an upturn may be slight in any given situation. No matter. No one can take the responsibility for assuming it cannot happen. To do otherwise is to hold history in contempt." He is right!

TOOL BOOK

APPENDIX A

Text References and Sources for Individual Research

ಐಐಚ

Chapter One
From Employment to Retirement

Text References

Dinesen, Isak, *Out of Africa*, Random House Inc., 1937. *Out of Africa* is the story of Isak Dinesen's life on her farm in Africa from 1913-31. It deals with the loss of property and love, as well as the courage it takes to survive and transcend them.

Walker, Margaret Urban, *Mother Time: Women, Aging and Ethics,* Rowman & Littlefield, Inc., 1999.

Sarton, May, *As We Are Now,* Norton, 1973.

Wingrove, R.C. Ray and Slavin, Kathleen, "A Sample of Professional and Managerial Women: Success in Work and Retirement, " *Journal of Women and Aging*, (3), 1991, pp. 97-117.

Conway, Jill, *Road from Coorain,* Alfred A. Knopf distributed by Random House, 1989. A narrative of Conway's journey from an Australian sheep-farm to the US and ultimately the presidency of Smith College.

Graham, Katherine, *Personal History,* Alfred A. Knopf, 1997. A great read for anyone interested in the role of women and the history of politics during the 1960s; 70s; 80s.

Markson, Elizabeth W and Taylor, Carol A., "The Mirror Has Two Faces, "*Aging and Society,* Cambridge University Press, 2000, pp. 137-160.

Furman, Frida Kerner, *Facing the Mirror: Older Women and Beauty Shop Culture*, Routledge, 1997.

Friedan, Betty, *The Feminine Mystique,* Simon & Schuster, 1963.

Cunningham, Michael, *The Hours,* Farrar, Straus, and Giroux, 1998.

Copper, Baba, *Over the Hill: Reflections on Ageism Between Women,* The Crossing Press, 1988.

Cousins, Norman, *Human Options,* Berkely Books, 1981.

Heilbrun, Carolyn, *The Last Gift of Time: Life Beyond Sixty,* Dial Press, 1997.

Friedan, Betty, *The Fountain of Age,* Simon & Schuster, 1993.

Pellegrini, Angelo. *The Unprejudiced Palate*, Lyons and Burford, 1948; 1984.

Schechtman, Marya, *The Constitution of Selves,* Cornell University Press, 1996.

Bauer, Maglin Nan, and Radosh, Alice, *Women Confronting Retirement,* Rutgers University Press, 2003.

Helpful Resources Not Cited in the Text

Blank, Thomas O., Rinehart, Alice Duffy, and Williamson, Robert C., *Early Retirement, Promises, and Pitfalls,* Insight Books, Plenum Press, New York, 1992.

Brown, Marie Annette, Robinson Jo, *When Your Body Gets the Blues: The Clinically Proven Program for Women Who Feel Tired and Stressed and Eat Too Much,* St. Martin's Press, New York, 2002.

Hall,Phyllis, *BonusYears: Women and Retirement,* Miranda Press, 2002.

Sadler, Jeri, Miner, Rick, *Don't Retire, Rewire,* Alpha, 2003.

Vaillant, M.D., George E., *Aging Well,* Little, Brown and Company, 2002.

"Women Seek New Models for Later Years Challenges" (includes caregiving, forging fresh ties) Series: New Outlook on Retirement," (all of the 11/13/97 Edition); Christian Science Monitor.

Chapter Two
From Salaries to Coins of Time

Text References

Johnson, Spencer, *Who Moved My Cheese?,* G.P. Putnam's Sons, 1998.

Price, Christine Ann, *Women and Retirement: the Unexplored Transition,* Garland Publishing, Inc., 1998.

Stone, Howard and Stone, Marika, *Too Young to Retire: an Off-the-Road Map to the Rest of Your Life,* The Writers' Collective, 2002. This reference is particularly strong in finding volunteer or part-time work. Chapter 5 lists 101 opportunities for the open-minded. The Stones can also be found on their website on Retirement: www.2young2retire.com

Fowler, Lynda K, "Understanding and Strengthening Healthy Relationships Between Adult Children and Parents," Ohio State University Fact Sheet. Website: http://ohioline.osu.edu/flm99/fs04.html

Bloom, Harold, *How to Read and Why,* Scribner, 2000.

DeBolton, Alain, *How Proust Can Change Your Life,* Pantheon Books, 1997.

Conway, Jill, *When Memory Speaks,* Alfred A. Knopf, 1998.

Helpful Resources Not Cited in the Text

League of Women Voters Web site includes information on a national level and ways to become involved locally. Many of our respondents indicated they were politically active and frequently participated in League work. www.lww.org

Young, Heather M, and De Tornyay, Rheba, *Choices: Making a Good Move to a Retirement Community,* Hignell Book Printing, 2001.

Carter, Jimmy, *The Virtues of Aging,* Random House, 1998. Carter's emphasis is on planning for retirement years and offers worthwhile suggestions for opportunities open to senior citizens, particularly ideas for volunteer work.

"Best Places to Retire," *Money Magazine,* June 9, 2003. Also accessible on the Web at Money.cnn.com

Sun City—Del Webb has communities for living designed for active adults in many states throughout the U.S. Information available on his website: www.delwebb.com

SCORE is an agency assisting volunteers with executive experience to help small businesses get started. Almost all communities have this in place. Website www.score.org; 1-800-634-0248.

Elderhostel offers intergenerational travel options both in and outside of the U.S. Website: www.elderhostel.org; 1-877-426-8056.

Generations United is a coalition of more than one hundred national organizations-including AARP, The Child Welfare League of America, the Children's Defense Fund, and the National Council on the Aging—working on intergenerational issues and programs. Generations Unlimited reports on intergenerational community service projects, featuring young and old people as equal teammates working together and strengthening cross-generational relationships in the process.

VolunteerMatch has as its mission helping everyone find a great place to volunteer. Website www.volunteermatch.org

Chapter Three
From the "Given" to the "Unknown" in Social Relationships

Text References

Sarton, May, *Journal of A Solitude,* W. W. Norton, 1979.

Morrison, Mary C., *Let Evening Come: Reflections on Aging,* Doubleday, 1998.

Taylor, W.E., Klein, L.C., Lewis, B.P., Gruenwald, T.L., Guring, R. A. R., and Updegraff, J.A., "Female Responses To Stress: Tend and Befriend, Not Fight or Flight," 2000. A study conducted at UCLA.

Waxman, Barbara Frey, *From Hearth to the Open Road: a Feminist Study in Contemporary Literature,,* Greenwood Press, 1990.

Bauer-Maglin, Nan and Radosh, Alice, *Women Confronting Retirement: A Nontraditional Guide,* Rutgers University Press, 2003.

Helpful Resources Not Cited in the Text

Jackson, Rachel W, *The Reading Group Handbook: Everything You Need to Know From Choosing Members to Leading Discussions, ,* Hyperion, 1994.

Many book publishers provide free Reading Group Guides wherever books are sold. Almost all have websites; e.g. www.readinggroupcenter.com Another Web site representative of most publishers is www.vintagebooks. com/read

Many community colleges across the country have "Gold Card" privileges for seniors which allow registration on a space available basis for a minimal fee (in Washington State that fee is only $5). Gold Cards may be obtained from the Information or Admission Office at your local college.

Communities nation-wide have a number of different hiking organizations frequently accessible through the web; e.g. www.trails.com For organizations go to www.hikingamerica.org Canada offers www.eldertrek.com which is similar to Elder Hostel but exclusive to trekking. In addition, there are countless outdoor stores that provide information about recreational hikes in their area. One such, initiated in the northwest, now nationwide, can be found at www.rei.com

www.mastergardeners.com offers national and local information about gardening.

Hal Taussif, *Idyll Untours* is an economical apartment-based European travel package which lets you experience a foreign country as an "insider" at your own pace. May be reached at www.untours.com; 1-888-368-6871.

Elderhostel provides opportunities for learning about a vast array of subjects in addition to providing structured comfortable travel options. The web site invites "insider," self paced exploration of foreign countries. Catalogs are available as well. www.elderhostel.org; 1-877-426-8056.

The Smithsonian Institution offers trips throughout the world. Log on to www.SmithsonianJourneys.org or phone 1-877-338-8687.

There are several Websites for Home Exchange. The Stones in *Too Young To Retire* recommend www.digsville.com because of its rating system. Service organizations such as Rotary International also sponsor such exchanges. An additional possibility is subscribing to *The Caretaker Gazette* at www.caretaker.org which offers maintenance, gardening, or property management rather than home exchange; 1-830-336-3939.

Video entitled *Not For Ourselves Alone*, a film by Ken Burns and Paul Barnes, produced by Florentine Films, 1999. An excellent record of the suffrage movement and the role of women in the late nineteenth and twentieth centuries.

Mungo, Ray, *Your Autobiography More Than 300 Questions To Help You Write Your Personal History*, Macmillan, 1994.

Pederson, Reda, *What Next? Women Redefining Their Dreams in the Prime of Life*, Perigee Books, 2001.

Chapter Four
From Professional Prompts to
Self-Generated Challenge

Text References

Cruickshank, Margaret, *Learning to Be Old: Gender, Culture and Aging,* Rowland and Littlefield, 2003.

Moody, Harry R, "Age, Productivity, and Transcendence," in *Achieving a Productive Aging Society,* Auburn House, 1993.

Erikson, Joan M., Erikson, Erik H., and Kivnick, Helen, *Vital Involvement in Old Age*, Norton 1986.

Gannon, Linda P., *Women and Aging: Transcending the Myth,* Routledge, 1999.

Nelson, Todd D, *Ageism: Stereotyping and Prejudice Against Older Persons,* MIT Press, 2002.

Cusack, Sandra H, and Thompson, Wendy J.A., *Leadership for Older Adults: Aging With Purpose and Passion,* Brimmer/Mazel, 1999.

Furman, Frida Kerner, *Facing the Mirror: Older Women and Beauty Shop Culture,* Routledge, 1997.

Chapter Five
How May We Know We Are
Leading the Good Life?

Text References

Mannes, Marya, *But Will It Sell?* Lippincott, 1964.

Berman, Morris, *The Twilight of American Culture*, Norton, 2000.

Waxman, Barbara Frey, *From Hearth to the Open Road: a Feminist Study in Contemporary Literature*, Greenwood Press, 1990.

Maitland, David, *Aging As Counterculture: A Vocation for the Later Year,* Pilgrim Press, 1991.

Fussell, Paul, *Class: A Guide Through the American Status System,* Simon and Schuster, 1983.

Freedman, Marc, *Prime Time: How Baby Boomers Will Revolutionize Retirement and Transform America,* Perseus Books Group, 1999.

Cousins, Norman, *Human Options,* Berkely Books, 1981.

Restak, Richard, *Mozart's Brain and the Fighter Pilot*, Harmony Books, 2001.

Helpful Resources Not Cited in the Text

Furman, Frida Kerner, *Facing the Mirror: Older Women and Beauty Shop Culture*, Routledge, 1997.

Many communities have athletic clubs that offer classes in tai chai, yoga, and pilates. Helpful Web sites include: www.gaiam.com

(excellent resource for yoga and pilates); www.yogadirectory.com (contains a list of yoga teachers, centers, organizations, retreats and vacations).

Although meditation is often included in yoga references, there are countless books on just meditation. An additional resource for meditation is located at www.aliveandhealthy.com

The Esalen Institute offers more than 400 workshops each year in a wide range of topics relating to mind and body building. Further information and/or a copy of the catalog is available at www. esalen.org

The Omega Institute is the nation's largest holistic education provider and is highly regarded for its pioneering work in holistic health, meditation, yoga, transformational psychology, spirituality, world music and art. Website at www.eomega.org

Primary Works: The Fiction of Aging

Adams, Alice, *To See You Again,* Penguin, 1982.

Laurence, Margaret, *The Stone Angel,*Bantam, 1981.

Lessing, Doris, *The Summer Before the Dark*, Bantam, 1973.

Lessing, Doris, *The Diaries of Jane Somers ,* Random House, 1984.

Marshall, Paule, *Praisesong for the Widow,* E.P. Dutton, 1984.

Pym, Barbara, *Quartet in Autumn*, Harper & Row, 1977.

Sarton, May, *As We Are Now,* W.W. Norton, 1973.

Sarton, May, *Mrs. Stevens Hears the Mermaids Singing,* W.W. Norton, 1975.

Taylor, Elizabeth, *Mrs. Palfrey at the Claremont,* Dial Press, 1975.

The above cited works of fiction depict middle aged women revisiting their past and imagining their future lives. In the process, they confront losses and adjustments and arrive at a sense of freedom and independence, allowing them to try out new roles. Love and death share equal space as the authors challenge prejudices and stereotypes of aging.

APPENDIX B

Questionnaire Summary

At the onset of our research, we sent out 36 questionnaires to elicit (1) the degree to which retired professional women had experienced the career rewards of salaries, intellectual stimulation, and social contacts; (2) the degree to which they missed those in their post retirement lives. We defined "retired professional women" as individuals who had worked continuously in their professions for at least 10 years. Our target audience lived in rural and urban areas across the country and represented a wide range of fields: education, health professions, business, accounting, law, and the arts.

Space was allotted for comments in each category; e.g. other satisfactions; and a final question addressed the ways in which respondents either had or would transform the career rewards of salary, intellectual stimulation, and social contacts into retirement values. This additional information proved as rich for mining as did the checks in designated rubrics.

*Significant Statistics Obtained from the
Returned Questionnaires*

Satisfaction from salary during professional lives:
42% checked GREAT
58% checked MODERATE
0% checked NONE

Degree of missed satisfaction from salary in retirement lives:
11% checked GREAT
55% checked MODERATE
34% checked NOT AT ALL

Satisfaction from professional challenges in career lives:
100% checked GREAT

Degree of missed satisfaction from professional challenges in retirement:
21% checked GREAT
47% checked SOMEWHAT
32% checked NOT AT ALL

Satisfaction from making social contacts during career lives:
63% checked GREAT
37% checked MODERATE
0% checked NONE

Degree of missed satisfaction from social contacts in retirement:
7% checked GREAT
47% checked SOMEWHAT
46% checked NOT AT ALL

APPENDIX C

Sources for Group Exploration and Activities

W*hen Professional Women Retire, Food for Thought and Palate* lends itself as a starter text to at least four different group explorations inviting participants to clarify and internalize identified ideas and issues via practical, hands-on interchange and activities.

These group encounters may be led by anyone with some experience in group leadership or may be conducted by Ellie and Inga who can be contacted at hjheff2@aol.com and iwwiehl@aol.com, respectively.

We suggest the following group gatherings: chautauquas, seminars, workshops, and focus groups depending on audience, purpose, and time commitment.

Chautauqua

For example, we chose the chautauqua format for a gathering of the women who had answered our questionnaires. They provided an audience with some knowledge of the topic—professional women's retirement issues —and shared our purpose of interchanging ideas and experiences and moving forward in our lives. In the spirit of a chautauqua, which "edifies and entertains," we proceeded in the following way:

I   Opening remarks to welcome the audience and state the purpose for the meeting.

II   Exercises for participants. Questions to be answered individually, in small groups and in the entire group, led by a facilitator.

Questions distributed and answered individually:

■ What do you like most and what do you like least about being retired?

■ Beyond good or reasonably good health, what three things in your life make you feel grateful?

■ If we understand "ageism" to mean "discrimination and prejudice against older persons," when and where do you see or have you seen it in your own experience? When and where have you observed it in that of others?

Facilitator divides participants into groups of two or three (depending on numbers) and gives instructions to share individual responses. Facilitator records what they wish to share with the entire group, indicating similarities and differences of responses.

III Break for Refreshments

IV   Summary:

A. Each group shares summary responses with facilitator allowing questions and answers as appropriate.

B. Facilitator summarizes responses of entire group.

V. Evaluation: Facilitator distributes 5x7 cards asking participants to

A. Write down what they learned from this chautauqua. Indicate whether what they learned from this gathering suggested topics for further pursuit in subsequent chautauquas, or other types of group meetings.

Our chautauqua lasted three hours, which seemed about the right amount of time for the task.

Seminar

For a different occasion with a different purpose, we would conduct a seminar. We have been approached by a retired university faculty organization to give a presentation on retirement transitions and plan to lecture there on the moves from employment to retirement, salaries to coins of time, "givens" to "unknowns" in social relationships, and professional prompts to self-generated challenge. The audience in this group may be any number of people with or without knowledge of the topic, but generally curious enough to attend the meeting.

Individual involvement in a seminar is most frequently optional. The amount of time spent is regulated by the confines of a regularly scheduled meeting, one and one-half to two hours, which makes the seminar format suitable to the agenda of any organization.

Workshop

A workshop may start out with a brief presentation, but unlike seminars, workshops demand individual participation and substantial time commitment. Workshop participants come not only to explore a given topic but to work toward a goal in terms of formulation and development of methods for reaching it. They meet with the understanding that the workshop will offer tools for future explorations. The first part of a workshop frequently lays the groundwork of clarification and formulation of objectives; the second would focus on implementation in terms of action steps.

A workshop may last one or more days depending on the tasks. Activities may include means of self discovery such as personality tests, interest tests, true colors test, Meyers-Briggs evaluation, and "dream catchers" exercise.

One or more of those may be followed up with exercises on goal setting and subsequent action steps.

Focus Group

The purpose of focus groups is to elicit opinions among a representative group of people about a variety of issues in politics, education, business, or community outreach.

For example, a new senior citizen center is opening in your community and you feel strongly about its purpose being other than merely care giving or bowling. In addition to those, you would like to promote individual efforts toward enriching the lives of older citizens, in terms of setting individual and collective goals and taking positive action.

To advocate your cause, you might set up a focus group to determine the direction and means of reaching your objectives. Focus groups provide qualitative data not available from other sources, such as surveys.

Focus group activities are highly structured, and time commitments for participants are generally limited to one and one-half to two hours. The burden of success rests on the individuals who design the questions to be addressed by the group, select group representatives, and conduct the analysis of responses. Consequently, of the four kinds of group activities, focus groups are the most demanding in terms of leadership and may require professional guidance.

Given a professional life of conducting these four learning experiences, we know that they are neither exclusive nor "pure." Methods of presentation and kinds of group activities may be interchanged. All of them may also invite follow up meetings and activities. Seminars, for example, may lead to a follow-up chautauqua or workshop in which attendants would want to offer active participation and come prepared to make contributions based on the information gleaned from the seminar.

ABOUT THE AUTHORS

Inga Wiehl holds a BA from the University of Copenhagen and an MA and PhD in comparative literature from the University of Washington. Following her husband's career in the FBI, she taught at the University of Washington, University of Utah, Westminster College, Utah, the University of Texas, and Centralia Community College before moving to his home town of Yakima, where she was employed as an English instructor at Yakima Valley Community College. Her years of teaching there were interspersed with two writing sabbaticals, as well as one quarter at the University of London as a professor for American Students Abroad. In 1993 she won the Leadon Award for Excellence in Teaching and in 2003 received the Faculty Emeritus designation. In addition to her teaching, she served three two-year terms as a speaker for the Washington Commission for the Humanities and accepted a five-year assignment as administrator and project director for the Faculty Development section of the college's Title III grant. She has written articles for Danish and American journals related to her discipline as well as contributed thirty monographs on Scandinavian women in the arts, literature and politics to a *Women in History* series issued by Yorkin Publications.

Ellie Hefferman graduated *magna cum laude* and Phi Beta Kappa from Knox College with a B.A. in political science and was subsequently awarded a fellowship to study and teach in the Maxwell School of Citizenship at Syracuse University. She received her M.A. before marrying and moving to Georgia with her husband. In Athens she taught political science for five years at the University of Georgia. Her husband's internship moved them to Illinois where she taught at North Central College. Upon moving to Yakima, Washington she worked part-time at Yakima Valley Community College as a teacher and counselor while her children were young. As she returned to full-time work, she became Director of Counseling, Registrar, and subsequently Dean of Students. Upon retiring, she served a year as an interim Dean at Bellingham Technical Community College. As a counselor, teacher and dean, she has worked with countless returning women students and in the process acquired substantial knowledge as well as a keen interest in the lives of professional women. She has served on numerous statewide committees and twice made presentations at the American Association of Community and Junior College national meetings based on articles submitted to journals in her field. Additionally, she has been responsible for writing and editing the college's schedule, catalog, advisor's handbook, and student orientation packet.